SHOUT THEM FROM THE MOUNTAIN TOPS II

Georgia Poems and Stories with Art & Photos

Jean B. Copland, General Editor
Hildegard K. Holmes, Editor
Jane Dillard Knight, Editor
John S. Knight, Jr., Editor /
Production Manager

A Project of the
Georgia Council of Teachers of English

Printed in the United States of America

ISBN (Paperback) 978-0-9632498-3-8

Shout II Book Design
Gerald Boyd
GCTE Treasurer/_Scribbles 'n Bits_ Co-Editor

Photography and Cover Design for _Shout II_
Jim Cawthorne, President, Camera 1
www.camera1.net**, Columbus, GA**

Brad Wheeler - Graphic Layout and Printing
Diversified Printing – www.1dps.com Columbus, GA

iii

Table of Contents
Poems & Stories

Introduction, Dr. Jean Copland viii

Dedication ix

Acknowledgements x

America, Eugene F. Elander 1

Eden Lost, Barbara K. Lipe... 2

White River, Arkansas 1989, Tom Liner 5

Animal Whimsy, Carroll Edward Lisby.. 6

Hide and Seek in the Tennessee Aquarium, Cathy Maze 7

Fortune, Ellouise Connolly 8

Curses, Foiled Again, Emery Campbell.. 9

Mama's Magic Wand, Jacqueline Lawrence Keller.................... 10

Eve' Pea Patch, James R. Whitt 12

What Was, Patsy Hamby.. 17

Night Phantom, Jane Dillard Knight 17

O So Much to Do, Jane Dillard Knight 17

A Gift for You, Jean Copland 18

Messages, Jeanne L. Koone 19

The White Dog, John C. Berlin.. 20

The Killing Stone, John R. Handy 22

A Bluebird, a Poppy, and a Dragonfly, Kathy Wright 25

Silent Hero, Robert L. Lynn.. 27

A Balm of Life, Mary O. Lisby.. 28

When it Rains, Nagueyalti Warren.. 29

A Week with Grandma, Merrill J. Davies................................... 30

First Spring in Georgia, Sandy Hokanson.................................. 31

Rock Garden, T. L. Hensel.. 32

The Willow Tree, Carroll Edward Lisby..................................... 33

The Ghost of Me, Jason Wright 34

Pier Pilings on Fernandina Beach, Cathy Maze 35

Today, Cathy Maze 36

Memorial Day, Emery L. Campbell.. 37

In Our Universe, Eugene F. Elander 39

Our Special Place, Jacqueline Lawrence Keller........................... 40

Saved by the Flare, Emery L. Campbell 41

Beyond the Glass, Susan F. Boyter 45

August Rain, Kathy Wright.. 46

The Daily Commute, Jeanne L. Koone 47

Semantics, Mary O. Lisby.. 48

What's in Your Cup?, Kathy Wright 50
In the Country Walking, Nagueyalti Warren 52
Christmas Eve in Henryetta, Robert L. Lynn 53
A Skinny Dipping Adventure, Michael Whitt 54
Thank You, Rufus Horace Adams, Mary O. Lisby 59
Winter Woods Walk, Jane Dillard Knight 60
Coach Mora Shows the Rookies Around the Hereafter, Steven Shields 61
Absentee, Susan F. Boyter 62
On the Banks of Sabbath Creek, T. L. Hensel 63
Jitterbug, Blackbirds, and Hula-Popper Sparrows, Susan F. Boyter 65
Radishes, T. L. Hensel 66
Recovenanted, Barbara K. Lipe 70
The Old Ship, Nagueyalti Warren 71
The Road, A Destination, Sandy Hokanson 72
Old Mountain Dreamer, Rosemary Dixon 73
An On-Going Conversation, Anderson Frazer 74
Where a Poem Comes From, Ron Self 75
Lasting Friendship, Brenda P. Dixey 76
The Poetic Process, Jane Blanchard 77
Lying Together, Anna Nero 78
Where the Rats Live in Piles, Renee Basinger 79
Oktoberfest, Gerda Tarkington-Smith 80
Cousin Willy and the Killer Hairbrush, Anderson Frazer 81
Spoons, Don Gerz 84
Bicycle Breeze, Lynda Holmes 85
Third Snow, Hilary King 86
Underneath Magnolias, Hilary King 86
Spring Gossip, Hilary King 87
Homonyms, Synonyms, and Momma'nems, Freddie O'Connor Riley 88
Got This at Goodwill, Freddie O'Connor Riley 89
About the Author, Jacob Martin 90
In My Psalm, Jacob Martin 90
Memoir, Jane Blanchard 91
Daddy's Brain, Anderson Frazer 92
The First Glimpse, Anna Nero 93
Firestorm, Mary A. Gervin 96
Fire Ants, Mary A. Gervin 97
Adrenalin Junkie, Mary A. Gervin 98
A Breeze, Mario R. Mion 98
The Layover, Gerda Tarkington-Smith 99

Meditations on a Flame, Jacob Martin 103
Oh, What a Day, John Ottley, Jr. 104
Get God in Your Game, John Ottley, Jr. 105
December in Atlanta, J. C. Reilly... 106
Late Summer Music, J. C. Reilly 108
5Ever, J. C. Reilly 109
The Gig, Steven Dunn.. 110
Fallen, Steven Dunn... 110
Legacy, Judy F. Brouillette 111
Yard Sale after the Funeral, Judy F. Brouillette..................... 112
Déjà Vu, Judy F. Brouillette.. 113
Possibilities, Jessica Nasca.. 114
the garden, Kathleen McKenzie 119
Bridges, Lavonda Forbes... 120
Traveling through Georgia, Kathy Nichols............................... 122
Cold Comfort, Lisa Stafford.. 127
Manna, Lisa Stafford.. 128
Fall, Lynda Holmes 129
Hula Hooping, Lynda Holmes 130
In My Dreams, Nancy Lawson Remler...................................... 131
Incognito, Nancy Lawson Remler.. 136
The Other Half, Jason Wright 139
The Harvest, Nell McWilliams 140
Dinner Date, Phyllis McCoy Lightle.. 142
Zookeepper's Pantoum, Phyllis McCoy Lightle 142
Ridge Road, Phyllis McCoy Lightle 143
Old Teacher Man, Mary Reid 144
Arkansas Pine, Renee Basinger... 145
Fly Me to the Moon, Ron Self.. 146
Poem Read Aloud, Ron Self 147
Crossing the Fall Line, Sandra Giles....................................... 148
First Memory, Sandra Giles 149
At the Aquarium, Sandra Giles 149
Just Past the Yellow Sign, Shane Wilson................................. 150
Merry Christmas, Mr. Crowe, Mary Reid 153
The First Time in Years, Merrill J. Davies............................... 157
The Journey, Ellouise Connolly.. 161
White Lies, Like Snowflakes, Jason Wright 164
Daddy, Patsy Hamby... 165
So Many Miracles, Eugene F. Elander..................................... 166

Art & Photo Gallery

Yates Mill Pond, Diane Osborne 167
Lizard on Bamboo, Alisha White 167
The Guardian, Peggy Albers..168
Tintern, Kristen Hansen 168
Thames Path, Kristen Hansen 168
Western Jekyll Sunset, Kathleen McKenzie 169
Butterfly, Alisha White..169
Lizard on Birdhouse, Alisha White..169
Contemplation, William South 170
Eiffel Details, Barbara Lipe 170
Bath, Kristen Hansen 170
Savannah Statue, Patricia Gerard...171
Artistic Dogwood, Betsy Hollis-Frey 171
Waterfall, Brandi Mazesticeon-Hamson 171
New Day on Jekyll, Kathleen McKenzie 172
The Old Church, Sidney Wilson 172
Savannah Cemetery, Patricia Gerard 173
Azaleas, Herb Cawthorne 173
SWtheCloudCrowd, Geri M. Davis..173
Jekyll Island Sunrise, Kathleen McKenzie 174
Mountain Castle, Sidney Wilson 174
Savannah Fountain, Patricia Gerard..174
Only in Venice, Geri M. Davis 175
Southern Winter, Sidney Wilson 175
Descanso Gardens, Roseanne Marie Peters 176
Watermelon Delight, Teresa McCullohs..176
The Art Lesson, Geri M. Davis...177
For Cotton, Diane Osborne 177
Ice Queen's Cave, Sidney Wilson...177
Clematis, Herb Cawthorne..178
Bill Brought Me Roses, Roseanne Marie Peters 178
Touching Trumpets, Diane Osborne 179
Wash Day Break, Diane Osborne 179
In Hog Heaven, Diane Osborne 180
Let Sleeping Dogs Lie, Teresa McCullohs 180
Roadside Graveyard, Teresa McCullohs..180
West Georgia Sunset, Diane Osborne..181
Horseshoe Rock, Brandi Mazesticeon-Hamson...............................181
Amidst the Carrot Field, Peggy Albers 181
The Four Editors 182

Introduction

Shout them from the Mountain Tops II has been produced as a second *Shout*, following *Shout I*, 2003, both sponsored by the Georgia Council of Teachers of English, a non-profit State organization of English Language Arts educators, to promote and support the world of art and education, with emphasis on poetry, short story writing, art, and photography.

This GCTE project also began with a question as did *Shout I* with the question from my friend and editor, Jane Dillard Knight, "Why don't we write another book?" With *Shout II*, the question was from GCTE President Kathleen Rose McKenzie, "Will you do another Shout?" Again, the response was "Yes, with the help of *Shout I* editors".

When requests for submissions to *Shout II* were broadcast in various ways, with periodic announcements on the *Shout II* link to the GCTE website, and with the help of other organizations, hundreds of submissions came in via email and US Mail. The GCTE Board asked for stories to be included with poems; then art and photography were added. "Georgia Poems" became "Georgia Poems and Stories with Art & Photos". All works included are original, never before published poems, stories, art, and photos.

Contributors who currently live in Georgia submitted a plethora of ideas, some with Georgia scenes or reflections, requiring a "Random" design to accommodate the various, ideas, and styles. The book opens with poems and stories with the color art and photos featured in the "Art & Photo Gallery," also organized in random fashion.

It is important to note that this project, sponsored by GCTE, is entirely non-profit in that no one, including contributors and editors; book and cover designers, paid fees or received payment for their contributions. All contributors keep their copyrights to their works and must be contacted for any use of their material.

Once more, we "Shout Them from the Mountain Tops!"

Jean Copland
General Editor, et al
jcopland@mchsi.com

Dedication

Shout II is dedicated to poets and writers;
artists and photographers living in Georgia and
in the entire world for sharing their creative
works, which perpetuate imagination, literacy,
and the arts—
with a spotlight shining on each *Shout II*
contributor.

Acknowledgements

Shout II has received bountiful contributions and support for its production for which we, the editors, are grateful. We will start at the beginning with the person who thought it would be a good idea to produce another *Shout*: President Kathleen Rose McKenzie of the Georgia Council of Teachers of English (*Shout II* sponsor). "Thank you, Madame President, for your idea, and thanks to the GCTE Board for their support!"

All other former *Shout I* editors, Hilde K. Holmes, Jane D. Knight, and John S. Knight, agreed to be editors again; Selection Committee Chairs agreed to be responsible for the selection of poetry, stories, art, and photography: Tom Liner for poetry and stories; Geri M. Davis for art; John S. Knight, Jr. for photography, along with other members of the committees who helped with the selection: Kathleen Rose McKenzie, Katie Greene, Jim Cope, Anna Lee Nero, Brenda Logan, and Kathie Haney. Thanks for your major contribution to another *Shout II* accomplishment.

Appreciation goes out to Kim Knight, GCTE Publicity Chair, and groups including the Georgia Center for the Book, Georgia Poetry Society, Brick Road Poetry Press, and Columbus Branch of the National League of American Pen Women; also, to Columbus Artists' Guild, Pine Mountain Poets, family, friends, and strangers for promoting and encouraging submissions to *Shout II*.

We have all of you to thank for your efforts in promoting *Shout II* and for your support of its production.

We are much obliged to Gerald Boyd, GCTE Treasurer/Co-Editor of *Scribbles 'n Bits*, GCTE newsletter, for the book design and to Jim Cawthorne, President of Camera I, Columbus, Georgia, for his photography and cover design of *Shout II*.

Shout II **Editors**
Jean B. Copland
Hilde K. Holmes
Jane Dillard Knight
John S. Knight, Jr.

AMERICA: September 11

Tune: America the Beautiful

Oh Beautiful, through darkened skies,
Through tragedy and pain
Yet, through it all, our prayers still rise:
They have not died in vain.
America, America, sometimes our path is hard;
Yet, we'll not fail, right will prevail,
With faith in Thee, and God.

Oh Beautiful, for heroes all,
In building or on plane;
For those who answered to the call,
Whom we'll not see again.
America, America, sometimes our path is hard;
Yet, we'll not fail, right will prevail,
With faith in Thee, and God.

Oh Beautiful, for all that's good,
Our best is yet to be;
We reaffirm our brotherhood,
From sea to shining sea.

America, America, sometimes our path is hard;
Yet, we'll not fail, right will prevail,
With faith in Thee, and God.

-Eugene F. Elander

Eden Lost

Eden buttoned her cuff, studying her image in the mirror. The face that frowned back belonged to someone vaguely familiar, someone she no longer really cared to know.

She turned and spied a framed snapshot, leaning against a stack of books on her dresser. Light rays spilling between window blinds illuminated a man's face, sun-browned and smiling at her, a face Eden loved. She smiled back and remembered all the times she had watched that face beside her at the table, from across a room, above hers in a disheveled bed. Her heart began to churn. Her throat constricted painfully. Tears clouded her vision. She reached for the door frame.

"What an absurd old woman!" she spat at herself and stepped into the hallway. Large red numbers from the clock on the bookshelf warned her: 12:00, 12:00, 12:00.

"Oh, I'll be late," she whispered, rushing into the kitchen, gathering up her purse. At the back door, Eden rummaged for her keys in a shallow pewter bowl. "If I leave now, I'll be there before 12:30 and surprise him," she spoke aloud as if someone listened.

Eden stepped out and locked the kitchen door, checking twice to be sure that the lock held. "Can't be too safe can we, Harold?" She felt rather than heard his agreement as she planted first her right foot, then her left on each of three steps down to the sidewalk, and let herself out through the gate.

The sun hung low on the horizon to the East. A trick of light? Eden fished sunglasses from her purse. "Much better," she murmured, striding toward the corner of

Albertson and Fifth, then heading across the intersection without a thought to traffic.

As she walked to the bus stop, Eden was propelled by a sense of the importance of her destination — a date with Harold for lunch. She considered what they'd order. Harold loved the café on the square. Today was ... Tuesday, so it would be fried chicken, or if she was wrong about the day, what did it matter? For the second time this morning her heart quivered.

The sharp shushing of bus brakes startled Eden. When the door folded open, she stepped up, took a quarter from her wallet and offered it to the driver. The young man stared at her hand and then looked into her eyes. "Tokens are a dollar, ma'am."

"I've never paid that much before!"

He shrugged.

She could walk the rest of the way, but she'd be late. Eden tugged a dollar bill from her wallet, unfolded it and handed it to the driver. He accepted it without looking up, and she grabbed a handhold as she sidestepped to an empty seat. She had only time to sit and arrange her purse on her lap, when she looked up and saw familiar buildings ahead. The bus bumped to a stop.

A young woman in front of her with the most amazingly red hair turned and helped Eden down from the bus. She smiled at Eden and said, "There!" Then, they walked without speaking in the same direction as far as the corner of Bull Street and Main. There the young woman turned to Eden as if to ask her something, but shaking her head thought better of it and called, "Have a nice day, ma'am," as she hurried away. Eden watched until the red hair disappeared into a building halfway down the block.

At her empty house on Albertson Street, Eden's phone rang five times. When the answering machine clicked on, an electronic voice droned, "No one is available. Please leave a message at the tone."

"Mother? This is Evelyn. Mother, please pick up. It's 9:15. I'm running a little late, but I'll be there in ten minutes ...to take you to your doctor's appointment at ten. Be ready."

The voice sharpened, "Mother, please answer me. Are you there? Mother, where are you?"

The machine beeped again as it broke the connection, and a dial tone was the only answer Evelyn received.

Eden crossed the street. The windows of the building to her right were painted over in black. Why had Harold played this trick on her, inviting her to this strange place? How would she ever find him? Her chest began to ache as she slumped against the dusky glass.

She bowed her head and concentrated on breathing.

When she looked up, a young man stood beside her speaking quietly, asking her name and where she lived, as if she were a child. "I'm supposed to meet Harold," Eden explained through sudden tears.

"Don't worry ma'am," he soothed, taking her arm. "We'll get you home."

She resisted. "But what about Harold?"

-Barbara K. Lipe

White River, Arkansas 1989
a photograph for Tommy and Daniel

the river is behind us
cold and moving
we smile and laugh, ready
for the boat and the current
to the shoals, stepping down
the long day in the sun
fog ghosts over the water
soundless in morning light
there are fish here
big fish

it is the place of healing
we stand together as
fishermen, father and sons
holding the long rods of our
longing together
smiling at the camera
and thinking of fish

we will fish
thighdeep in cold water
Roundhouse Shoal, Wildcat Shoal
the Narrows and the Rim
flylines like scribbles on the sky
out there drifting with current
the bright speck of a fly
lost to sight and found by
something fast as the color
of light, strong as the river
beautiful as hope
we are here
and the day and the fish
have come to meet us
in this place of the river
together at last   -Tom Liner

Animal Whimsy

Pretty little crocodile,
Watch him frolic, see him smile.
Pretty little crocodoo.
His next dinner may be you.

The octopus enjoys
Playing table tennis.
With his eight arms
He always winnis.

The giraffe's behavior
Beats me to heck.
He's just not one
To stick out his neck.

The zebra's color
Is strange, alack!
Is it black on white
Or white on black?

The gator's short legs
Deter his romping,
But his big jaws
Are great for chomping.

The graceful hippopotamus
Trips the light
Fantasticus.

When the buzzard flies
A commercial jag,
He always packs
A carrion bag.

I've never seen a unicorn
Frolicking in the mist.
But that shouldn't be surprising
Since they really don't exist.

-Carroll Edward Lisby

Hide and Seek in the Tennessee Aquarium

In the dim aquarium light
a flash of silver darts
through underwater forests,
plays hide and seek in sea grasses
undulating in slow motion. Images
of pilot fish and manta rays diving
to the tank bottom fascinate
a four year old, fill him with endless
questions easier to answer than ones
from which I cannot hide.

Just for this hour, I long to be
as he is, full of joy, unmindful
of planes exploding into skyscrapers,
unaware of people jumping from windows
high above Manhattan. I want to forget
how terror drowns New York
in ash and concrete, pretend
the aquarium's small shark
has no counterpart in my world.

Tonight I will see fear
and disbelief reflected on the faces
of young children, and begin to fathom
that even they are not spared.
But for this precious time, I hide
from unspeakable truths
already broadcast around the globe,
just for this moment, I crush memories
of assassinations, of missiles,
of what happens when evil plays
hide and seek with civilization.
I hold my grandson close, put my face
against his soft, warm cheek, and briefly
see the world through his eyes.

-Cathy Maze

Fortune

From words found in a fortune cookie, a strip
of paper, the challenge was to compose a poem.
Words pulled from the inner folds of the cookie tugged
at my mind, tossing it to a sixteen year old girl holding
her hand out for the gypsy woman at the State Fair, and
hearing her foretell, "You will live a long life". She
did not say I would eat many fortune cookies.
Staring at this strip of paper I am aware her prediction
is surprisingly accurate.
I have not thought of that day in years as in a
sudden flash my mind turned to that long ago enduring
summer ritual at the fairgrounds. The exhibition buildings
displaying needlework, arts and crafts, canned goods and
recipe judging booths with my winning potato salad.
Game booths, death defying sideshows, horse racing, ferris
wheels and merry-go-round all grabbing for attention.
The ancient science of fortune telling by the veiled woman
who analyzed the marking on my hand with a great deal of
pomp and ceremony only brought giggles from a sixteen
year old. Sixty-five years later this small amusement brings
reflection as I realize my life has been small strips of paper,
pulled one at a time from
the fortune cookie of life.

-Ellouise Connolly

Curses! Foiled Again

Prince of Darkness and the son of God
each thinks himself more gifted in the use
of his computer. Jesus says, "You clod,
you're clumsy as a rearing, roaring moose.

"I'm much the best at plying my machine."
"Oh no you're not," says Satan. "I'm the best."
But God is not amused. "I've never seen
such irksome quibbling. I can get no rest.

"We'll have a two-hour test, then I'll decide
the winner. I can't stand it any more."
So Jesus and the Evil One abide
by God's command to wage computer war.

They use the mouse, they fax and e-mail, too.
They download, send attachments, write reports
containing charts and graphs. They also do
hard spreadsheets, labels, letters, and all sorts

of projects, deal with problems that they pose,
face all the hi-tech issues that exist.
Lord Jesus is a whirlwind, heaven knows,
and Satan's fast as hell, no detail missed.

The testing time is almost at an end
when sudden thunder rolls and lightning streaks
the sky. As these conditions often tend
to do, the power's cut as lightning peaks.

The Evil One is stunned, then screams and swears
because his screen goes blank. He's livid, raves,
"My work is gone! I've lost it all!" He glares.
His rival's calm. God shrugs, says "Jesus Saves."

-Emery L. Campbell

Mama's Magic Wand

My Mama was the first person I ever knew who owned a magic wand. Its powers, never ceased to amaze me. My first memory of it came about when I was very young. We lived near a swampy lake and had strict orders not to go near the lake. One day I was drawn by the lure of the forbidden and decided to take a walk by myself around the lake. What could it hurt? It was only about a block from our house.

Happily, I went skipping along the banks of the lake, softly singing a refrain from a song I had heard on the radio. It was all about wishing, and my young heart was full of wishes. I sang the words I knew and hummed the rest. . .I remembered the refrain, "If you just wish long enough, wish strong enough, you will come to know, wishing will make it so." My wants and needs were simple, and I wanted so much to believe the words of this song. I did believe them.

Fantasy reigned as I drank in the sights and sounds of this forbidden territory. I stopped short as I came upon quite a magical, storybook place. Leaning over slightly, I peered at an old, moss-covered concrete drain. A pipe under the bank channeled water through, and it trickled from the pipe into a great, square, concrete receptacle, greenish and stained with age. My eyes followed the drops of water as they fell through it, then into the lush undergrowth below to become part of a creek that just ran on forever. I could feel the magic, just as I felt when I read in my storybooks of moss-covered gates and such things in hidden, secret gardens. I sat there and wondered where the creek went as it journeyed away from the lake. My young heart was filled with things of the imagination, wonderful magical things. In fact, these musings of mine were what introduced me to Mama's magic wand.

10

As I knelt over the old drain watching the water trickle down, I was completely lost in my thoughts. Suddenly, I heard my name spoken ever so faintly. My attention caught, I strained my ears, and I heard my name again. "It must be some sort of water nymph calling to me," I thought. Imagination—wishing—could make it so, and in rapt anticipation, I turned around as I heard the creaking of a twig behind me on the path of the bank.

There stood my Mama, and in her hand was her magic wand—her keen little switch—and she moved it toward my legs. "I was worried," she said, all the time waving the magic wand. As she moved it, I began to dance around, and I could see many things. My Mama loved me very much, and I had frightened her. No "you're grounded," no "you're restricted," but Mama's wand spoke volumes. With a few sweeps I knew beyond a doubt what the wand was telling me.

I'd like to say that this was the last time I learned from Mama's magic wand, but what I can say is that each time she used it, I learned a lesson that stayed with me for life.

That was a long time ago, and now, many years later, I have my own magic wand. It's perfect! It's keen, supple, and just strong enough. In fact, a magic wand bush grows right in my backyard. I can break one off easily. Why just today, I introduced my energetic and headlong, little grandson to its magic powers. He understood instantly and became a believer. My Mama was a wise woman, and when she spoke, I learned to listen.

-Jacqueline Lawrence Keller

Eve's Pea Patch

(As told by one who personally witnessed the events here reported)

"I was born about four thousand years ago
There ain't nothin' in this world that I don't know
While Adam and Eve were eatin'
From the bushes I was peepin'
I can swear that I'm the one who ate the core"

(A little ditty my father often sang. Origin unknown.)

Early one bright morning a long time ago in a place called Eden, Eve emerged from her humble abode. It was her custom the first thing upon arising each morning to stroll in her vegetable garden in order to clear from her head the cobwebs of the previous night' s repose. The cool morning air always refreshed her and brought her sensitivities to full alertness. This was before the invention of Mr. Coffee.

On this particular morning, she noticed, immediately upon exiting the structure which she called her house, that the storm which had passed through during the night had deposited a huge limb from a nearby tree on the very ground she had the day before so diligently prepared for planting. She had high hopes for a fine crop of peas in this section of her garden. Now, however, the presence of this fallen limb looked to hinder her hopes. She began to wonder if her desired pea patch would become a reality.

After surveying the situation for a few minutes, she decided that she would have her breakfast and then simply move the limb so that she could plant her seeds as she had planned. She turned and went back to her kitchen to fry some bacon and eggs.

Knowing that moving the limb would require a sturdy breakfast, she cooked herself an extra rasher of bacon and two eggs instead of her usual one. Also, she fixed herself some blueberry pancakes and topped them with sour cream and some delicious blueberry syrup which she had concocted only the week before. Thus fortified for the task which lay before her, she grabbed her garden gloves and headed into her garden determined to remove the pesky limb.

Eve walked up to the limb, grabbed hold of it with both hands, and gave a mighty tug. The limb did not budge. She got hold of it from another angle and again gave a mighty tug. Again the limb did not budge. She backed off and studied the limb for a short while in order to determine its center of gravity and where it might be most likely to give in to her efforts. Then she attacked it yet once again. Yet once again, the limb held steadfast to its mooring in her planned pea patch. She called it a few choice names hoping it might succumb to humiliation. Then she tugged again. The limb was not in the least humiliated, nor did it respond to her agitated efforts. The limb was going nowhere and Eve had gradually slipped from determination to agitation, and was gradually approaching the very verge of desperation. However, Eve was many things but there was one thing that she was not, and that was a quitter. She spent the entire morning trying to remove the fallen limb from where she wanted her peas to grow.

By mid-day Eve was completely exhausted. She had pulled, pushed, lifted, tugged, and kicked. She had beseeched, cursed, cajoled, and demanded. At one point she had knelt calmly beside the limb and begged it to please get up and remove itself to another location so she could plant her peas. The limb appeared not to even hear her plaintive plea. All of her efforts had failed. It was a stubborn limb.

In her struggles she had stumbled, tripped, and fallen. She had skinned her knees and elbows. She had red whelps on her forearms where the branches protruding from the limb had broken the skin. Little rivulets of blood flowed from her wounds and trickled down her shins and arms. She scarcely noticed. The limb, however, was as fresh as when she had first laid hands on it some several hours before. It looked to be no worse for the struggle, and it had not moved one inch from where the storm during the night had placed it.

Eve took a break from her toils. She had been at constant battle with the limb all morning and had not even halted to catch her breath. She stood back from her adversary and thought, "If I only had a chainsaw". But, like Mr. Coffee, chainsaws had not yet been invented either. She considered giving up and preparing a new bed for her beloved peas, but something inside her held fast to that particular spot. It was the perfect spot for peas to grow, and she so desperately wanted them to be there. Tears began to swell in her eyes and roll down her cheeks, mixing with the sweat that had already run from her brow to her chin.

It was about this time that she heard a voice calling her name. She turned and looked in the direction from which the voice came. There, standing at the edge of her garden, having emerged out of the nearby forest, was the Creator. She stood proudly before the Creator, tears, sweat, blood, effort, skinned knees and all.

"Eve, my child," the Creator asked, "what is wrong?" In a flurry of emotion with her hands and arms waving, and with blood, tears, and sweat flying, Eve explained to the Creator her predicament.

The Creator listened patiently. When she was through and all her frustrations of the morning had been put into words, she relaxed and fell silent.

The Creator looked at Eve with deep empathy and

14

spoke. "Eve, I am very proud of you. You have been a good steward of my creation. Your garden is beautiful. You have accomplished all of this of your own power and ingenuity. You have asked for nothing. But I can see that you are in need of assistance. So I am going to create a helper for you."

Eve was taken aback. "A helper," she asked, "what's a helper?"

The Creator responded, "This helper that I am going to create will be very much like you in form. There will, however, be some differences which you will find amazing and grow to like and enjoy. Your helper will be bigger than you and much stronger in stature. Your helper will be able to move that limb for you without even breaking a sweat.

Eve was all excited. She loved living in Eden but she often got lonely and wished she had someone to talk to and with whom to share the trials, joys, and pleasures of her sojourn. She was tingling with anticipation of a helper when the Creator interrupted her ecstasy.

"There will be just one condition," the Creator spoke.

Timidly Eve asked, "What's that?"

"Well," the Creator answered, "this helper will not be able to bear fruit, as you can, to replenish the Earth. Your helper will therefore suffer insecurity. Also, your helper, unlike you, will be slow of thought and will therefore, in an effort to reach equality, place excessive value on that which is thought as opposed to that which is felt. Last, because of these differences we will have to let him believe that I created him first."

And so it came to pass that by the time Eve laid her weary body down to rest that night, the pesky limb had entered into the realm of history, and she had planted her peas exactly where she wanted them to be. She had decided to call her helper Adam, and discovered that the difference

15

in form of which the Creator had spoken really was quite amazing, not even to consider the ease with which he had dispatched the limb. As her eyes gently closed in slumber, a contented smile swept across her pretty face.

"Yes," she whispered, "quite amazing indeed!"

Adam had gotten up and was sitting at the table. He was busy drawing up plans for Mr. Coffee and a chainsaw. Between sketches he was racking his feeble brain trying to think up new words, somehow believing it was his solemn duty to name everything.

Addendum

I cannot take sole credit for the origin of this tale. I read a brief two paragraph version of it many years ago in a newspaper. I cannot speak to the report of any other witness, if indeed there was one. This is the way I saw it.

I cannot take credit for Mr. Coffee or the chainsaw. I did not invent either one. However, I have one of each. Mr. Coffee is my resurrection each morning. After that, I stroll the vegetable garden.

The chainsaw was left to me by my father. I take good care of it and am pretty darn good at using it. My wife, Michael, grew up in central Florida where there is scarcely anything known as winter. Where we now live, when the temperature dips below 50 degrees she wants a fire in the fireplace. That chainsaw and I, plus my axe and pesky limbs that summer thunderstorms drop, keep her supplied with firewood all winter. It is hard work and I enjoy doing it because I love her. Love has a way of rendering even the most arduous tasks pleasurable.

Michael is also very fond of peas.

-James R. Whitt

What Was

(A poem based on a rural Georgia scene in one of the fastest growing counties in the United States)

There was no four-lane divided highway through here back then
When couches and chairs in that house were full of folks.
And adults bantered around the table,
While children chased each other through the rooms
Or nestled in their beds.

No more quilts hang on the clothesline now
And all the roof shingles have blown away.
The six brick pillars no longer support a porch
And only a few pieces of grey siding remain
While a piece of weathered plywood bars the front door.

And the raging bulldozers destroy flower beds
And scrape down to the stone
While they shove green grass into ugly red dirt mounds
To lay the foundation for a gated community
Where the home once was.

-Patsy Hamby

Night Phantom
Owl cries from the tree
then sends its black shadow
to fly over me.

"O so much to do"
Feathers all awry
Titmouse stops to rest
From building spring nest.
-Jane Dillard Knight

A Gift for You

I brought you a gift,
A gift from the sea,
Hot vermilion
With streamers of purple,
Pink, and blue,

Shot through with silver
Streaking out like flying
Ribbons fluttering and floating
Above calm water lulled and hushed,
Waiting for the memorable moment

Hot vermilion glides slowly
Out of the sea casting deep red blushes
Against the horizon …
In a moment your gift will shine
Its red glow hot and bright

Into your eyes and warm you,
Rising up slowly, slowly,
Then, up fast, suddenly
In your face …
How do you like your 6:30 sunrise,

So bright and hot, welcoming
You to a new day,
Gifting you with light?
Hold on to the glow!

-Jean Copland

Messages

All Hallows Eve
and high sails the moon;
whispers the breeze
a faint haunting tune.

Tremble the leaves
on the orchard trees,
paint lacy patterns
in a shadowy frieze.

Swift sigh the spirits;
free for one night;
ride with the wind;
such is their right.

Brush at the window,
slip under the door;
they know the right places;
they've been here before.

Some say they pass
soft as a fawn;
murmur a message;
by dawn they are gone.

-Jeanne L. Koone

The White Dog

I was disappointed as I walked away from our job of replacing the foyer glass in a home. My associates hardly noticed my departure, but I was sorely depressed.

I had failed to correctly measure a large, critically central piece of beveled glass, and we were going to have to come back in two weeks with the corrected work.

No one said a thing to me because I owned the tiny company. No one would want to embarrass me with my own ineptitude. I was supposed to be the expert, you know, the grand master.

As I wandered through the empty house, I haphazardly slumped into a sofa in the den. It looked like the right spot for me to feel sorry for myself. I almost never made this kind of error and, to make matters worse, the people with whom we had this contract were my best friends.

Something bit into the rear of my ankle. I lurched forward just in time to see a tiny puppy flying across the room in search of its next intrigue.

The puppy was all white and might have weighed three pounds. It threw itself on top of a red rubber toy and noiselessly ripped the leg off. I rolled a yellow and blue tennis ball across the room. The puppy's nose and eyes throttled up in full tracking position and launched at immediate top speed to head off the tennis ball trespass. The attack was so ferocious that, as it bit into the top of the ball, the puppy flipped over backwards – her rear end slamming into the wall nearby. *Was that wall interfering with matters of the great hunt? This cannot be tolerated.*

The puppy spun around and bit the wall, which, knowing its place – kept silent. She spied the crate which was not only her home, but the repository of delightful distractions purchased by her humans.

She charged into the open crate and threw out a decapitated giraffe and then selected a piece of rope with a large knot in it. The knot would not come undone: clearly intolerable. Leveraging with both paws, she pushed the knot away as the other end suffered in her teeth. She killed it, giving it the famous dead-snake shake which is buried somewhere in puppy DNA, and then noticed I had rolled yet another ball.

In a surprise move she charged the ball but then ever so slightly changed her direction and, in two bounds, was upon my ankle again.

My laughter filled the room and my heart with the simplicity of living life on its own terms and not mine. This puppy was teaching me more about seeing the joy which God intended than I could ever grasp on my own.

And I pondered that I might not ever lose one more moment of my life to unhappiness.

-John C. Berlin

The Killing Stone

Yes, as he drove closer he was now sure buzzards were in the tree. So there was trouble. The Farmer got out of the pickup truck as the hill slope was too slippery for the vehicle, and slowly walked in the drizzling rain toward the tree. The footing was slick; there were skid marks left by the cows as they slipped on the wet red clay of the hill. He saw a bale of hay with its enclosing piped ring, but no cows were in sight. A blur of reddish brown appeared beside the ring, and he knew an animal was down. As he approached the tree the buzzards flew off, and he went to the downed animal. It was a two to three hundred pound heifer, lying on her side. Walking slowly, the Farmer approached the animal, who made no effort to arise. The expected scurrying, retreating haste of a healthy calf was not present. The heifer's head turned back over her body as she watched the Farmer, the wet red clay coating part of her fur, as if the struggling animal had slipped about in the mud. The left front leg was angled abnormally with a great protrusion of the shoulder. The Farmer knelt and gently felt of the shoulder, the heifer making no movement. It was obvious the shoulder was broken with a flail leg. She somehow must have been caught in the hay ring, breaking the limb in her struggles to free herself.

The Farmer quietly entered The Daughter's room. She was lying on her side, the ventilator quietly and rhythmically puffing. He pulled up a chair and sat facing her with her unseeing eyes slightly open, the ventilator tube entering her neck.

In the months following the accident, killing his wife and maiming his only child, his initial hope of her recovery had been slowly and reluctantly replaced over the months by despondency, but finally an acceptance of the permanence of her brain-dead state. Speaking softly to her, he pulled back the sheets and gently stroked the thin, unfeeling arm. An intravenous line was in the veins of her arm with an attached hanging bottle — unusual, because feedings and drugs were normally passed by the tube through her nose into her stomach.

The Farmer knelt a long moment, watching the heifer, wondering what to do. He knew if the animal did not rise, the buzzards would start their feed even as the animal was still alive - pecking out eyes and anus first. It was too great a distance to drag the heifer to his truck, and even if he could have so done he had no way to heft the animal into the truck bed. The hill was too slippery to bring the truck to the heifer, and night was falling and the drizzle was increasing. The Farmer carried no gun in his truck but did wear a sheath knife. He was not sure he could bring himself to slit the heifer's throat. In looking round, half buried nearby was a large irregular stone — perhaps the size of a melon. He rose, dislodged the heavy stone from the clay, and holding it with both hands stood at the calf's side, looking down at the still animal. The Farmer then slowly raised the heavy stone above his head, hesitated a few seconds, and with the stone's weight and all of his strength brought the stone crashing down onto the calf's head.

As The Farmer sat staring at his daughter, The Doctor entered, pulled up a chair, exchanged pleasantries with The Farmer, and with his chin in his hand watched The Daughter for a long moment with no further talk between the two men. Then, speaking softly as to be barely heard by The Farmer, The Doctor said, "You noticed the bottle?"

"Yes," answered The Farmer.

Speaking even lower, so The Farmer had to lean a bit to catch the words, The Doctor said, "There's a lot of

23

potassium in that bottle. Her blood potassium was a little low this morning."

A faint crunching sound like that of walking on fresh snow accompanied the blow, and the heifer's body jerked as her eyes rolled back in her head. The Farmer partially stooped, watching, a feeling of deep desolation and sadness rising in his mind, but the animal continued to breath and jerk. Twice more The Farmer quickly again raised the stone above his head and sent it crashing downward onto the calf's head, each time again hearing the crunch. After the third blow the breathing and jerking stopped, and blood began to trickle from the heifer's nose. The Farmer stood motionless, staring at the still animal. He then quickly straightened, arched his back, threw back his head, thrust his arms with out-stretched hands toward the sky and looking upward into rain with his face contorted with anguish cried to the empty country-side - "God, forgive me!"

There was a long pause; then, The Doctor continued, "If the bottle were to run in quickly, it would poison her heart, and she would immediately die, painlessly."There was another long pause and nothing further was said by either man. The Doctor rose and with an impassive face shook The Farmer's hand and left.

The Farmer sat for a prolonged period of time, watching The Daughter. He then rose slowly and stood at her side looking down at her thin, unseeing face, his fingers touching her arm. His gaze then lifted to the bottle, and as he watched, the bottle seemed to assume the shape of a stone.

-John R.Handy

A Bluebird, a Poppy and a Dragonfly

I used to think when someone reached retirement age they were old, but now that my husband and I fit in that category, I prefer words like "seasoned" or "mature" when referring to retirees. I also once embraced the mistaken thought that anyone age sixty-five and up, had little more to do than to leisurely meander through his or her remaining days. How wrong I was regarding both ideas. What I've learned since is that today's Seniors are some of the busiest people on the planet. We truly are active adults, trying to be the best we can be.

Always keeping a finger on the market's pulse, the pharmaceutical, fashion, and cosmetic industries have been busy too, churning out appropriate product lines that echo Hillary Clinton's 2008 campaign declaration that *sixty* is the new *forty*. Because we are indeed living healthier and longer lives, rather than a cushioned rocker on the porch, more and more of us are finding that retirement is brimming with opportunities to broaden one's horizons, to learn new things, to get involved in community affairs, to travel, and to volunteer.

With this new sense of enlightenment percolating in my brain, I recently received three photographs (via the internet) from my good friend, Jane. The first picture was that of a bluebird, the second—a single red poppy, and the third—a tiny, iridescent blue dragonfly.

"I'm having way too much fun with my new toy," Jane wrote. "So long since I've had a camera, I feel silly and giddy."

As I looked at the picture of the bird, frocked in handsome blue feathers, I could almost hear his come-hither serenade. Regarding the poppy, I thought the flower was wellnamed—its color so intense that the red popped, even on the computer screen. Last, I studied the dragonfly.

With the tip of my finger resting on the insect's image, I traced over the shape of its long, thin body and diaphanous wings. "How small and beautiful you are," I whispered, "a living, breathing streak of indigo, perched on a blade of grass."

I once heard it said that a picture is the hostage representation of a person, place or thing—fixed in time—once and forever frozen in the moment. Again, looking at each photograph, I began to think about what an incredible world we live in and how fascinating it is to occasionally see part of it captured within a small frame.

I love that my husband and I are past those hustle-bustle, harder-working years of our lives and that we have more time together. I'm thankful that we're relatively healthy, busy and still eager to try new things. Nevertheless, basking in the illuminating light of my autumn years, I'm learning that being *too busy* can be a danger at any age.

As much fun as it is to experience the novel and new, to go and do, there is much to be learned in quiet times—in being still—in gifting one's self with unhurried moments in which to glimpse some small measure of this world's splendor as well as one's place within it. My friend's pictures are a reminder of how ironic it is that even in this computerized, digitized, warpspeed existence of ours, it's through the simple lens of stillness that we begin to discover not only the infinite wonder of a thing, but also our ability to enjoy it.

-Kathy Wright

Silent Hero
(Shakespearean sonnet)

My older brother volunteers for war;
He wrestles fighter planes from flattop deck,
An Okie lad on hail of bullets tour,
From Japanese assault his land protects.
A skilled, intrepid pilot he becomes;
His Grumman Hellcat bests the Zero's speed;
Our county daily heralds the outcomes
Of his dogflghts, his aviator deeds.
We siblings revel in heroic feats,
Cheer over bravery, citations won,
The missions he an ocean grave defeats,
Eluding tracing bullets of Nippon.
At home, of war, he whispers not a breath;
The young hero's still haunted dodging death.

-Robert L. Lynn

A Balm of Life

Bring me tea olive when I die. Not carnations that smell of death or other blossoms that have no smell at all, blossoms that have never seen the sun. It takes the warmth of the sun to bring fragrance to a bloom. Roses smell sweetest when the sun is full upon them.

Bring not tea olive but the smell of tea olive that lingers and perfumes the surrounding air. The smell that first alerts you that the shrub is blooming, for indeed, though my bush was planted many seasons ago, its bloom was always unexpected to me. Later I was told that it bloomed every month with an "r" in its name. I remember it blooming in the heart of winter when light snow sprinkled the evergreen leaves or icicles hung from its woody branches. The white flowers are so small and nearly hidden by the dark green leaves that you are awed that something so tiny can put forth such a vast amount of flavoring for the air.

Bring not the smell of tea olive but the memory of the smell. The memory of the way I planted the bush by the kitchen door so that with every going in or coming out I would be surrounded by the haunting fragrance and would take it with me to near places but far distant in the mind. I never went to many far away places. Some near places though, to me, were as difficult to face as climbing highest mountains or conquering other equally exotic challenges. Maybe much more difficult, and the memory of the smell of tea olive comforted me. Just as the smell of the tea olive will always remind you of me and you will be comforted by my love for you.

You don't remember the tea olive? Then go and find some and don't delay. Ephemeral though it is, it will give both ballast and balance to your life and is necessary for your journey. The search will bring you completeness so that you also can someday say, "Bring me tea olive when I die."

-Mary O. Lisby

When it Rains

When it rains she still mops and waxes the floors,
but she puts down newsprint for us to walk on.
When he comes in he always walks around
the paper careful not to put his muddy work boots
anywhere but on the cleanly shined floor, then he flops,
dust rising from his overalls, into the easy chair,
kicks his black lunch pail across the room and sighs,
damn they try to kill a man.

She won't make him take off his dirty shoes or walk
on the paper. Can't he see that she has worked all day?
Starched and ironed the kitchen curtains white, rubbed
down the windows with vinegar? Can't he smell the neck-
bones stewing in the pot? She has to bargain with the stingy
butcher to get fat ones and what about the hot cornbread
and pinto beans she sets before him and she doesn't even
make him wash his hands or use a napkin.

He cuts an onion raw into his beans and smacks his lips,
his whiskers brown with bean juice. *How was it today?* She
asks, ignoring his elbow on the table. *Same as every damn
day. Man don't you see this here child? Don't talk like that.*
The only time she ever scolds is for me but he never listens.
Mostly when I think of him I don't remember the dirt boots

or his ill manners, just his only swear: *Damn!*

-Nagueyalti Warren

A Week with Grandma

Thinning gray hair pulled back in an untidy bun,
With straying hairs falling on her short neck,
She was known as "Aunt Julie."
On hot days we'd walk through her flower garden,
Past rock wall and on to the store.
Cold "pop" and candy were worth the long walk.
Late afternoons we'd work with Grandpa in the garden.
Grandpa hoed tomatoes carefully and reverently.
Grandma hoed beans fast and carelessly.
Grandma shared with me her strong opinions about people.
("He's something the cat left covered up in the wood pile!")
I responded with giggles; her petite, pudgy body shook.
Her round face reddened with laughter at our private rhetoric.

Grandma had twelve kids and nearly forty grandchildren.
(But I was her favorite.)

-Merrill J. Davies

First Spring in Georgia

They bloom the end of April, someone told us.
So, winding up Neels Gap in the fog,
we drove north in search of dogwoods.
Then as sun broke through,
a million muslin knots
like a passel of women with rag-rolled hair
peeked out of the forest canopy
standing shyly amid tall pines and red cedars.
Mile-after-mile-after-mile of dogwoods
nodded, waved greetings as we drove by,

until we finally parked
and went in search of them on foot.
We followed the cadence
of falling water into dim forest,
led by lace-winged butterflies
skimming the tops of trilliums,
but found no dogwoods, only laurel leaves
in these deep woods. So we spent
the afternoon cataloging wild flowers,
watching water sluice over granite,
retracing our steps along muddy clay pathways

to our car. Soon after, we found a rustic store
full of marmalade cats and homemade jams,
When does mountain laurel bloom? we asked the owner.
Sometime in June, he said.
Usually the first of June. So we cruised
on down the Blue Ridge wilds toward home,
singing country songs along with the radio,
mapping out other Saturdays,
satisfied with the state of things.

                                    -Sandy Hokanson

Rock Garden

Your green thumb ambition surprised me
after the Peonies' death. The Peace Lily,
thoughtfully sent on Mother's Day by
our eldest, survived through hardy
resuscitation after each infrequent
watering. Regardless,
we journeyed on Georgia's gravel roads
far into the mouth of Appalachia
whose breath: deep and mossy,
wild and tangy with minerals -
stirred us as an innocent, but fond touch.

Into the streams you waded
to find and carry stones
turned and rounded by rushing water
formed from the hundred dribbles
off the hundred rocky chins.

We rested over sandwich and drink
keeping still our minds and movements, until
trout hidden by overhanging rhododendron
swam out to feed. Twelve, revealed,
living in the shallow pool.

Back home, you placed
and positioned each stone, its best
side established, and then as refinery:
Vinca, Hosta, Red-fox Speedwell,
Lavender, Sage, Oregano, Rosemary,
Our mountainside, our meditation garden,
our chipmunk playpen, our rabbit buffet,
below our porch from which we survey
Suburbia, while the evening bird and cicada
call down the night, as they
have done for millennia.

-T. L. Hensel

The Willow Tree

The willow saw
The King pass by
On the dark road
To Calvary.

She saw the thorns
Upon his brow,
The bleeding back,
And wondered how.

She saw the nails
That pierced his hands
And struggled hard
To understand.

She saw him die
Upon the tree
To save poor souls
Like you and me.

These things within
Her heart she keeps.
And that is why
The willow weeps.

-Carroll Edward Lisby

The Ghost of Me

Go ahead, pop another pill. It might
dull the pain, but it won't ease your mind or
exorcise your haunted memories. I
know I prey on your sanity. I know
you just can't let me go. But whose fault is
that? If you could have swallowed your pride as
easily as you down Valium and
Zoloft things might have been different. I could
have forgiven you. Maybe I would have
taken you back, but you just couldn't say
the words. Are you finally ready to
admit you made a mistake? I told you
the others wouldn't measure up to me,
but you had to have your way. You followed
your capricious heart and a parade of
wannabes and losers from Miami
to New York, but the only things you have
to show for your vast experiences
are an empty bed and shattered dreams. Once
upon a time we could have worked it out,
but you sold the rights to your fairytale
ending a long time ago. I've since moved
on to a better place, far away from
you and miles past the point of no return.
Now that you're drowning, I won't be there to
rescue you before you go under. You'll
cry victim all the way down until you
finally hit the bottom, but you don't
have anyone else to blame but yourself.

So go ahead, take another handful.
Those lipstick red Seconals might help you
sleep but, for as long as you live, the ghost
of me will never let you rest in peace.

-Jason Wright

Pier Pilings on Fernandina Beach

October sunlight bathes in gold
sea oats swishing atop sand dunes
as wine mellowed voices
drift from a weather-beaten deck,
merge with whispering surf,
with clicking fiddler crabs
skittering among broken shells,
mingle with the call of sea gulls,
the distant laughter of children.

Late afternoon shadows
play games with lounge chairs,
while ocean breezes dash grains of sand
against wobbling beach bags;
incoming tides bobble
a deserted fishing pole
beside three objects rising
from the sand like sentinels.

Slowed to the pace of island time,
old friends stroll unhurriedly
along Fernandina Beach
to discover ancient pilings
uncovered by recent storms,
enduring remnants of a forgotten pier
long ago washed away,
an old boardwalk where someone
stood to watch a sunrise,
amber pink then reddish orange,
not unlike this morning's first light.

Shaped by tides seen and unseen,
divergent paths return us time and again

to Fernandina's familiar shoreline,
where old friendships are ancient rhythms
of surf and sand, forgotten destinies
revealed as new discoveries,
where breakers tumble smooth
the rough edges of broken sea glass
and an angel wing cartwheels in sea foam,
vanishes, then reappears in the next wave,
where the sea constant ever changing
pulls us into her timeless dance.

-Cathy Maze

Today

Today flowed
from beyond time
past clouds and angels
came to rest
at the edge of the sea
where breakers sloshed
at my feet
where wet sand glistened
in the setting sun.

Today flowed on without
a backward glance
leaving the gift of memories
out beyond the horizon
and curled quietly
within my heart.

-Cathy Maze

Memorial Day

Ranks were forming in front of the high school for the parade at 10:30 a.m. Men and women encased in freshly starched shirts and dresses, farmers in their town suits, jackets over their arms; it was hot and humid. The columns would come down the hill, turn right at the Civil War cannon at the foot of the bridge, go up Fourth Street past the library, and on to the cemetery.

A bugle sounded: the parade had begun. Heat shimmered from the pavement in an ochre haze of dust. Drummers beat out a crisp cadence, steps were firm and quick.

Then a siren. The marchers looked at one another, then back toward the fire house. Losing form for a moment, they continued with hesitant tread as the band played briskly on. Whispering crept through the crowd, and finally one word rose above the excited hum: drowning! A few people broke away from the parade route and hurried toward the river. After the band, still blaring a Sousa march, had passed, those standing near the bridge moved onto it and stared down to where Thunder Creek runs into the Chattahoochee. A wooded tongue of land at the junction of the streams was a favorite swimming place for the town's children. A group had already collected on the point watching a boy shoulder-deep in the water fifty yards off shore waving his arms and shouting.

"Here, here, Joey's here!" sobbing, ducking under, coming up coughing. "Quick, get him, he just went down!"

"Come on out, boy. The sheriff'll be here with the boat directly, come on out." The balding little man advanced to the river bank, careful not to step in the mud with his spit-shined shoes. "Come on, son."

37

A second man in a too-tight Legion uniform joined the other on the bank and bellowed, "Get the hell outta there, kid! You're gonna get drownded, too!"

More watchers gathered, solemn, questioning, their clothes bright splashes against the river's dull placidity. Orange and black band uniforms stood out from the green trees and grass. A young woman in a yellow silk blouse pushed through the growing crowd. "Forrest, Forrest! Come up here to me!" She was slender and white. "Come here or I'll tell your mother."

The boy's face contorted with sobs. He dove under again, the sun sparkling on his wet bottom. "I touched him! He's here! I touched him!"

The young woman hovered on the bank. "Shame on you, Forrest, swimming without a suit! Wait till I tell your mother!"

The paraders had broken ranks and were streaming toward the point. The crowd on the bank stood immobile, rigid.

The sheriff, silver star emblazoned on a dark blue shirt, rowed down the creek from the power house dock. Spectators started shouting directions to him, but he seemed to ignore them. As he neared the frantic boy he threw out a grappling hook with a flourish, then hauled it back in, hand over hand.

The boy screamed at him, "No, no! Over here!!" but he threw the hook again.

Then a tall man thrust through the futility of watching faces. Shedding trousers, shirt, and shoes he plunged into the water. The men standing at the river's edge glanced at one another, shamefaced. With powerful strokes the swimmer reached the boy, dived, resurfaced, dived again. Eyes and uniforms watched. Finally, he came up gasping, holding the small naked body. On the bank polished shoes scuffed the powdery sand.

The onlookers stood quietly as the rescuer tried to revive the small form, forcing air into the boy's lungs. The man's heavy breathing was the only sound now.

Then someone coughed, breaking the silence, and edged away from where the rescuer worked over the lifeless child. The crowd murmured and began to straggle back toward the bridge.

-Emery L. Campbell

In Our Universe

In our universe, this is quite unclear:
Is there intelligent life, any place but here?

While it may contradict common sense,
We have yet to find any evidence,
That other species with intelligence,
Fill the universe with their sapience.

Our radio telescopes search the skies,
But no organized signals can they apprise;
Meanwhile, we beam signals of our own,
In the hope that humanity is not alone:
The law of squares, the value of pi -
Is the galaxy listening, standing by?

Could it be that we were heaven-sent?
Or is life but a cosmic accident?
Did lightning strike Earth's chemical stew,
With the ultimate result being me and you?
Then, soon, will evolution move on,
The human species to be gone?
Then, this question I must ask in fear:
Is there any intelligent life down here?

-Eugene F. Elander

Our Special Place

It is spring, and we stroll arm in arm to our special place in
the park—a place of beauty amidst tall, graceful
trees, perpetually green, but spectacular in
spring when love blooms.

Pristine, white, fashioned with intricate design, a delicate dowel-
studded bridge spans a mirrored pond—a bridge for
lovers—a special place.

Spring-flowering trees, bursting with blooms, can be seen all
around as we stand on the bridge where it arches gently
to a center rise.

Complementing each other, the crisp magnolias clothed in dark
greens lift tall branches over the bright green fringe of
the willow's slender branches that drift and trail in the
breeze.

The waters of the mirrored pond, with ivory-petaled water lilies
encased in snug beds of broad green leaves, appear as a
sparkling sky blue.

Bright flecks of sunlight spark off the curious gold fish darting
lazily about near the surface briefly, before hastening on
once again.

Feeling the oneness of young lovers, we linger on the rise of the
bridge, savoring each other's presence, and the beauty
that surrounds us, in our special place.

-Jacqueline Lawrence Keller

Saved by the Flare

We took off from NAS Jacksonville at twilight of a warm spring day in 1948. A red-orange flush still lingered in the west where the sun had disappeared, but the runway lights already gleamed. The wing and tail lights on our F6F Hellcat fighters cast a dim glow as the day faded. We made a wide circle over the field to join up and then headed south. The gathering haze and almost total cloud cover soon fulfilled their promise of a murky night; a cavernous blackness enclosed us before we had been in the air more than ten minutes.

Lt. Len Johnston, a short, austere veteran of a year's combat service as a carrier-based fighter pilot in the Pacific, led the first flight of four airplanes. We all knew Lt. Johnston felt wronged that the Navy had transferred him out of the fleet and assigned him the task of trying to make flyers out of "this bunch of plumbers," as he liked to characterize us.

I took off in fifth position and led the second four aircraft. The training syllabus at this stage dictated that our instructor introduce his seven fledgling midshipmen students to night cross-country missions, christened "group gropes" in the black humor of the day.

Pre-flight briefing had outlined a round-robin flight, one that did not involve a landing at our destination, Cocoa Beach, about one hundred fifty miles south of Jacksonville along Florida's Atlantic coast.

As second division leader I had to keep my four airplanes about twenty-five feet below and seventy-five to one hundred feet behind and to the right of the first four-plane formation. I edged in as close as the rules allowed and strained to keep the leaders in sight. Glancing back I could just make out the F6F on my left wing, a black mass punctuated by two eerie wingtip lights and the dancing blue

41

flames from its exhaust stacks. In my earphones I could hear the distinct "dit dah, dit dah, dit dah" of the south leg of the Jacksonville radio range, our aerial highway. My gaze swung back to the lights ahead and flickered down across the faintly glowing dials on the instrument panel to assure me that everything was in order there.

As we flew on and the haze began to lessen I relaxed a bit and dropped back to a more comfortable position relative to the formation leader. The lights on the ground, at first mere isolated pinpoints, became more visible. St. Augustine, a handful of glittering jewels on the earth's black velvet, drifted past off my left wingtip. I looked for Lt. Johnston's four-plane flight and saw their lights ahead, but they appeared much too distant. Berating myself for having lagged so far behind, I inched the throttle forward to catch up.

My situation did not alarm me, except that I wanted to get back in position before Lt. Johnston noticed my absence. I pressed on for a few minutes with my three division mates close behind me, but I still didn't seem to gain on the planes ahead. Anxious now, I increased my speed and leaned forward against my shoulder straps, keeping my eyes glued to the other formation's lights that appeared always to be just out of reach.

I boosted my speed for the third time.

Then my heart sank as Lt. J ohnston's voice reached my earphones. "Firebird five from Firebird leader, give me your position. Over."

"Firebird five," I replied. "About five o'clock from you, but I'm having trouble catching up. Over."

A silence followed during which I could imagine the lieutenant twisting from side to side in his cockpit trying to locate me.

"Firebird leader, I don't see you. I'll turn left so you can cut inside me and get back up here where I can keep you in sight."

I peered at the illusive lights and continued chasing them with renewed determination, but they didn't start moving left as they should have.

Then the horrible truth dawned on me. The "formation" that I could not catch didn't consist of airplanes at all but rather a group of stars glimmering in the distance! All the stories I'd heard about pilots trying to join up on lights on water towers or on automobile headlights moving along a highway came back to me. I had to let the flight leader know about my predicament, but how could I confess to such a blunder?

Ingenuity deserted me. I could only muster a sheepish, "I seem to have lost sight of you, Firebird leader. Over."

"A very shrewd observation," he drawled, ignoring our usual strict adherence to accepted radio voice procedure. He assumed a sarcastic, conversational tone. "And now if I may trouble you to make another observation, take a look toward the coast. We'll join up again at ten thousand feet over the beacon just swinging around in our direction. It should flash right about . . . now!"

I looked to my left as he spoke and saw several beacons along the shore at regular intervals. Just as he said "now" one of them flashed its beam in my eyes. I radioed that I had located the beacon and then turned toward it, scanning the sky for the other formation. We arrived over the appointed rendezvous site and began to circle. I searched the blackness in vain, for we still had this particular patch of sky all to ourselves. After a few more orbits it became all too apparent that I had added another faux pas to my evening's accomplishments by picking out the wrong beacon.

I cringed when the instructor's voice boomed out over the radio again. "I still don't see you, Firebird five."

I hesitated. Another beacon flickered about ten miles north. I turned toward it in desperation. This accidental stroke of luck brought tremendous relief for there, oh happy sight! were the other planes.

"Rejoining the formation, Firebird leader," I called as I slid into position.

"Firebird leader, roger. All right Firebird flight, we've had so much delay over this little reunion that we won't have time to go on to our destination. Returning to base. Out."

My uneasiness grew with every minute that passed. I knew that a tongue-lashing awaited me as soon as we landed. I could picture the instructor muttering to himself, refining a diatribe for my benefit. At last Jacksonville's lights shone beneath us. After an exchange of transmissions, the naval air station tower cleared us to land. Apprehension had me by the throat.

The lieutenant entered the landing pattern following the formation's breakup over the field. I watched with resignation as he made his final turn to line up with the runway.

Then two red flares blossomed in the air. At the same moment the tower operator's voice came over the radio. "Plane in the groove, take a wave-off! I say again, take a wave-off! Your wheels are not down!"

Neglecting to lower the landing gear as one prepared to set down constituted one of the cardinal sins of flying. A special watchman with a spotlight and a flare pistol always monitored night landings to check the undercarriage of each oncoming aircraft.

Perhaps too engrossed in rehearsing the abuse he intended to heap on my head, Lt. Johnston had indeed overlooked lowering his wheels. I could only speculate as to whether this explained his lapse. In any event, when the lieutenant, who had finally landed last, stalked into the hangar where we awaited the usual post-flight debriefing, he bade us a curt "Good night" and headed straight for the locker room.

He never again mentioned the evening's events.

-Emery L. Campbell

Beyond the Glass

She sits in tight-lipped silence in a frame
Of old gold leaf. Her nose is straight and strong.
Her eyes say melancholy things to me.
They warn that fifty-three is much too young
To leave her children and a spouse behind.
My father sits upon a stool beside—
A tiny boy, yet now he too is gone.

My mirror tells me she's alive in me.
I wonder if my grandchild, gazing long
At antique images in frames of gold,
Will feel a surge so strong.
I wonder too if sons will tell their own
The memories I'd choose for them to share.
I hope they'll say my tight lips poured out love.
Then, Ursula, I'll join you without qualm.

-Susan F. Boyter

August Rain

A mist, a sprinkle, a downpour,
I love the rhythmic opus of summer rain played out
on rooftops, its melody different somehow,
from house to house.

Ah, but when August folds and showers wane,
the requiem of May flowers floats on cooler winds,
after sunlit days shorten and leaves begin to turn,
after the dying season's veins lie exposed in the twisted
sprawl
of a shriveling tomato plant, in the broken backs of corn
stalks, plowed under.

A steamer filled with hot air, August is a fruit dropper,
a capricious waster that withers summer blooms
on the calendar's vine, a fickle month that doles
out a mélange of sun and heat and haze,
a time when wet weather doesn't believe in itself.

A mist, a sprinkle, a downpour or nothing at all-
August rain is unpredictable, unstable as a woman's tears.

-Kathy Wright

The Daily Commute

Oh, Thursday's drive's a storybook
of who's been where and who's done what.

Plantation X has partied well,
as overflowing trash cans tell.

A new dishwasher for Miz Kline,
the box states boldly "top of line,"

The Smith's new baby came as twins,
and Pampers overflow the bins.

Miz Brown's bag is small and light;
neighbors call it "the widow's mite."

Mangled suitcase, nine East Hadley,
Airline treated Joneses badly.

Were I a burglar, I could say
which summer homes are easy prey.

Those on vacation far away
have put no garbage out today.

The moral of this story then,
tell no tales to foe or friend.

So can it, bag it, tie it tight,
Keep the contents out of sight.

Borrow garbage from a friend
who will on trash day place a bin

Beside your drive while you're away,
confound the thief and save the day.

-Jeanne L. Koone

Semantics

Infantile paralysis
Paralysis
Poliomyelitis
Polio
Crippled
Paralyzed
Disabled
Physically handicapped
Physically challenged
Crippled.

A friend came with a joke to share: There was this tongue-tied man who had just returned from a world tour with his friend, Charley, who was disabled.

When he returned, he was excited to share his adventures. "We saw the Great Wall of China."
        An acquaintance asked, "Did Charley climb the Great Wall?"
"No, Tarley didn't climb the Great Wall.
"Tarley is twippled."

The traveler continued, "We went to England and saw the Tower of London."
        "Did Charley climb the Tower of London?"
"No, Tarley didn't climb the Tower of London.
"Tarley is twippled."

"And we went to France and saw the Eiffel Tower."
        "Did Tarley climb the Eiffel Tower?"
"No, Tarley didn't climb the Eiffel Tower.
"Tarley is twippled."

"Then we went to Italy to see the Pope."
"Could Charley go see the Pope?"
"Oh, yes. Tarley could go see the Pope. When we got there,
the Pope looked at Tarley and said,
"Trow away your right crutch
"And Tarley did."
"How wonderful! What happened next?"
"The Pope said, 'Trow away your left crutch'
"And Tarley did."
"Simply amazing! What happened then?"
"Tarley fell flat on his face. I told you Tarley was
twippled."

We laughed. Not for the attempt at humor but for the
reassurance
That we were still normal and could joke and tease among
friends.

Young then, we've lived with it fifty plus years.
Post-polio syndrome.

-Mary O. Lisby

What's in Your Cup?

Was it a hollowed out gourd or an upturned leaf? I'm not certain of their origin, but I think cups just may be one of the most useful and underrated inventions ever. Consider for a moment all the things we put into cups. A good place to start might be with the myriad ingredients heaped, poured and spilled into measuring cups. Tea is nice in a cup. Coffee's another popular choice, and a cup of soup or a cup of noodles are standard features on today's supermarket shelves.

I may be dating myself, but when it comes to cups and saucers, the first image that comes to my mind is that of the old Maxwell House Coffee advertisement and that well-known picture of a cup with a saucer and the memorable words, "Good to the last drop!" Still, nothing stays the same, and the once common cup and saucer has morphed into something today's folk call a "mug." My grandmother Morton would not have known what to do with a mug, That's because she and my grandfather made use of both their cup and their saucer.

My grandparents, like many of their family and friends, engaged in a peculiar Southern tradition known as "saucering,"
This was a custom I witnessed many times. I'm thinking of one particular morning. The sun had just begun to peek around the edges of the dotted·swiss curtains that hung at Nanny's kitchen window. Her noisy old percolator had finally finished its long, drawn-out song and dance, and a black iron skillet full of hot, buttered biscuits sat on the table in front of me. Beside the biscuits was an oval shaped platter filled with crispy strips of fried bacon and a large mound of soft scrambled eggs.

I remember Nanny washing my face and kissing my cheeks. "I sure love you, baby girl," she said, "do you know that?" Rubbing my still-sleepy eyes, I nodded in the affirmative. My grandmother then did a puzzling thing. She set her cup and my grandfather's to one side, picked up the shiny pot and slowly poured small amounts of hot black coffee into both saucers as well as both cups.

Today, I'm aware that freshly perked coffee is almost always too hot to drink. I also understand that hot liquid, poured into the flat base of a saucer, cools quickly. This is the custom my grandparents practiced while they waited for the coffee inside their cups to reach a proper drinking temperature. I can see them now, Nanny in her blue chenille housecoat and Granddaddy lackadaisically pulling up the straps of his overalls. Once again, I see them lift the shallow saucers to their lips, gently blow the dark redolent brew, and savor every sip.

Strange the things that stick in one's mind as a child, but it's not the memory of the odd custom of "saucering" that I treasure; it's the sense of *belonging* I felt in my grandparent's kitchen on that long-ago day when the golden light of morning rested on the window sill.

-Kathy Wright

In the Country Walking
Heat rises like a mist
liquefying the road before us
and flies swarm around
our bare heads.

Red dirt rises, sticks
to our sweat making us look
like the Maasai in Miss Adell's
coffee-table book.

Why won't the bus come this way?
It's too many ditches and pot holes.
Why don't they fix them?

She won't answer:
I'm mad. My lip pokes out.
She says, *Don't pout.*
Got something good for you
waiting at the house.

I don't care. I'm mean
eye-rolling wicked.
Good she doesn't see.

Inside shades drawn
it's cool and time for *Lassie.*
I sit on the footstool watching.
She gives me a green tin tumbler
filled with iced sweet tea.

I tell her Lassie just saved the day.
She can fix anything.
She says, *It'll take more than a dog*
to fix these Southern roads.

-Nagueyalti Warren

52

Christmas Eve in Henryetta

The band of ice shuttered the interstate;
we slid off at Henryetta
in front of America's Best Value Inn
and booked the last vacancy,
unable to reach our waiting, worried family.
Thus commenced the interminable night of highway snacks,
toasty naps, and the Christmas Eve broadcast of the
Mormon Tabernacle Choir.

As "Angels from the Realms of Glory" boomed,
I lifted the plaid window curtain
to uncommonly bright and swirling snow
as the young couple skidded up in their green Volvo
and occupied the rustic tool shed across the motel drive,

After midnight I spotted three guys
on their Harleys, smoking and genuflecting
outside the shed, their furry caps
mounding like shimmering crowns,
their faces cast as if they'd
just witnessed a roadside miracle.

We drifted back to family dreams
and next day rolled crustily on I-40
to celebrate with our loved ones
the birth two millennia back
in an animal cave in David's town
of Christ, the Lord, Emmanuel,
when some travelers like us
commandeered the only room left
with a window open to wonder.

                                        -Robert L. Lynn

A Skinny Dipping Adventure

Manda paced back and forth between Jen's bed and dressing table. As she moved, she repeatedly twirled a lock of her long curly reddish-brown hair around her right index finger. Jen was sitting on the bed filing her nails. Daphne and Carolyn were looking at Jen's DVDs for one of their favorite Eagle's records to play when the Springsteen album was finished.

"Do you think your folks are asleep yet?" Manda asked in a whisper.

Jen glanced at her watch, "I think so, Manda. It's after eleven".

"Surely we can make our escape if we're quiet," suggested Daphne.

"Let's give it a try," Carolyn agreed.

Manda watched as Jen unhooked the screen on one of the windows in her bedroom and slipped out. Then Manda sat on the sill and swung her long shapely legs out. She landed lightly on the ground. Manda and Jen waited for Daphne and Carolyn to follow. Manda fell in step with Jen as they tiptoed across the yard to Third Street. Carolyn and Daphne, giggling softly, followed behind them. When the quartet reached Third Street, they were only a two to three minute walk from Lake Silver, their destination.

Manda touched Jen on the arm and whispered, "Let's run the rest of the way." Manda and Jen began to run, followed by their two friends. They were at the lake in no time. Some of the lake property at the end of Third Street belonged to Carolyn's family. They could have gone swimming there but Manda had another idea. "Let's not go in at your place, Carolyn," Manda suggested, "We need the dock next door."

"I agree, Manda," Daphne responded. "If we put our clothes on the dock, we can get to them more easily if someone comes." Jen and Carolyn nodded in assent and the group trespassed on the neighbor's property. Soon they had all shed their clothes and were frolicking in the cool water.

"I love skinny dipping!" Manda exclaimed as she emerged from an underwater swim and propelled her tall, willowy form from under the water. "I love it almost as much as I love playing basketball," Manda continued as she came back into a standing position and splashed some water on Carolyn's long blonde hair.

Carolyn gave Manda a couple of splashes back and said, "Oh, Manda, we're going to be the best ever. And you're going to be the only sophomore on the first string next year."

"Yeah, we are," Manda replied. "And with you, Daphne, and me on the A-team, I doubt that we'll lose a single game." With that Manda splashed water with both hands on Daphne's shiny black hair. Daphne giggled right before her slender body disappeared under water.

In a few seconds Jen shrieked, "Ouch! What is that?"

"It's only me, Jen," Daphne replied as she surfaced laughing with pure delight.

"She pinched you, didn't she, Jen'?" Manda asked. "Next year when we're cheerleading together we will have to watch that brat. She's full of tricks."

"You'd better watch what you are saying, Manda Blake. If you don't, when I'm the editor of the yearbook and you are the assistant editor, I'll work you to death!" Daphne exclaimed.

The girls were gleefully wrapped up in their swim that nothing outside the immediate circle of their friendships entered their awareness. Nothing, that is, until they heard a male voice from the dock near the shore. It chuckled and then asked, "Well, well, what is this?"

They looked up and saw his dark form moving slowly toward where they had left their clothes, getting closer with every step. Each of the girls rushed toward the dock as quickly as she could, grabbed her garments, pulled them into the water, and frantically began to dress. While Manda was struggling to put hers on, she discovered with a sinking feeling that her bra was missing. She looked up and saw the intruder, John J. Harris, III, walking to his car with her bra in his right hand. In her haste she must have missed it, leaving it the sole item of clothing remaining on the dock.

"Johnny has my bra!" Manda gasped. She felt a sudden roll in the pit of her stomach as though she was going to be nauseated at any moment.

"Oh, no, Manda!" Carolyn responded sympathetically.

Manda immediately thought, "Why did this have to happen to me? I have the smallest boobs of anyone here. I wear a padded bra because I don't want to look as 'flat as a flounder.' Now, Johnny has that bra, and everyone will know." She paused a moment to look at her breasts and thought, they are just too small. The fact that they were perfectly formed in the shapes of two elegant teacups did not enter her perceptions. She looked up quickly and realized she had to do something. As she began to feel ever more desperate, she thought, "Maybe if Jen went and asked for the bra, he would think it was hers." Even though Manda knew Jen had breasts the size of grapefruits, she did not see that this would make it obvious that the bra was not hers.

"Jen, please go get it for me. Tell him the bra is yours," Manda pleaded.

"Manda, do you think that will work?"

"Yes, no, yes, um, I don't know. Oh Jen, please try it. I'm more embarrassed than I've ever been in my whole life." She could feel herself getting hot around the neck and face, and she was beginning to shake a little bit. She was quite undone by the situation.

"Okay, Manda, I'm going. Try not to be too upset," Jen said. Manda watched as Jen sauntered up to John J's car, and in a demanding voice said, "Give me my bra, Johnny."

John J. chuckled and replied, "This isn't your bra. I want this bra's owner to come get it."

Jen had done her best. Now Manda had no choice. She walked to his car maximally ill at ease. Her uncomfortable state was worsened when she saw her bra hanging from his car's mirror. She wished that she could miraculously disappear.

"Give me my bra, please," Amanda requested in a calm tone, although she felt anything other than serene.

Johnny smiled at Manda and handed it to her, "Okay, Manda. By the way, congratulations on being elected cheerleader. I know that Daphne and Jen are glad you're on the squad."

"Thanks Johnny," Manda responded. She could still feel her face and neck hot from blushing. She was now at the stage that she almost wished she was dead or at least comatose.

Until late Sunday afternoon Manda anguished about the teasing her small breasts and padded bra would bring to her. She knew she would receive plenty of it from Johnny's male friends at school Monday. Then she followed a strong impulse to take off her tank top and bra. Manda looked at her breasts in the full length mirror in her bedroom. For the first time since she had started comparing them to her friends, they looked good to her.

"I'm small, but I'm not flat, and my boobs are kind of pretty. No more padded bras for you, Manda," she said to her reflection in the mirror. "In fact, no more bras at all.

Jen needs one of the uncomfortable things. I don't!" The next day she went to school braless for the first time since the middle of the seventh grade. She would finish her freshman year in a couple of weeks.

Much to Manda's surprise when she went to school Monday, none of the dreaded teasing occurred.

"Hi, Johnny," Manda said to the young man as she walked up to him after lunch at his locker, "Bless you."

"Hi, Good Looking. Did I ever tell you that you have the prettiest blue eyes I've ever seen? And your blessings are welcome but what are you blessing me for?" Johnny asked.

"Because you're a great guy and I like you," Manda responded with a sunny smile.

It was Johnny's turn to blush. He looked at her with wide eyes and an enormous grin and gushed, "Gosh thanks. That means a lot to me Manda."

As she walked away, Manda realized that he truly did not know why she was blessing him. It never occurred to him to tell anyone about Friday night. Manda felt happy and relieved. She thought, "Johnny is a guy with real possibilities. He'll probably ask me out soon. If he doesn't, I might ask him."

                                                    -Michael Whitt

Thank You, Rufus Horace Adams

Thank you, Rufus Horace Adams.
I never met you but I have good reason to thank you.
I also know a lot about you:
You were older, not able to care for yourself at home,
And lived in a nursing facility.

I know you had a family who loved you and
Did what they could to ensure your physical
Comfort and well being.

I know all this because of a pillow.
Not like a couch pillow made for looks and not for comfort
and
Not a bed pillow or a store-bought one
But hand made with love,
Maybe by your wife or daughter or someone else who
loved you.
One to prop an aching shoulder or hurting hip or leg.
A pillow that is easy to move about to relieve aches and
pains
Wherever and give temporary relief.

For precaution, someone in your family
Had printed with permanent pen "Rufus Horace Adams" on
the back
So that it would not become misplaced or lost.

Why do I thank you?
When you didn't need it anymore, I saw the pillow at a tag
sale
For 50 cents, not even noticing your name on the back.
Why did I buy it? It looked comfortable and I took a chance
Because I also needed ease from hurting.

And the pillow helped.

We have adopted Rufus Horace Adams into our family.
We talk about you with familiarity and love and
Say you were always doing something to help
Somebody else all your life.

The pillow also serves well as a necessary bridge for
relationships
Between generations.
Thank you, Rufus Horace Adams.

-Mary O. Lisby

Winter Woods Walk

Brown and dry and curled,
a pair of winter leaves
circling close, whirling down
through bare brittle trees

Suddenly rise and circling still
Disappear from view.

Butterflies!

-Jane Dillard Knight

Coach Mora Shows the Rookies Around the Hereafter. One of Them Asks Where All the Buildings Are.

"There aren't any in Heaven, you know.
Never mind that part about the many,
mansions. You think that's literally true?

Don't be a dope. You aren't going to
need a house. What for? To keep your stuff in?
You think you're still going to have *stuff* here,

only nicer? A toaster that works for
a change, plush carpets, leather couch? A bed!
You think you get to *sleep*? You kidding me?

Who'd want to, even if it ever did
get dark. Which it won't. Maybe you expect
fine dining too, or maybe a double

whopper with bacon and cheese that wouldn't
clog your arteries? *Are you kidding me??*
ARTERIES?! STOMACH?! TASTE BUDS?? Sorry, don't

hold your breath. Or, do. It's okay. You don't
get lungs either, so knock yourself out. No,
really, you can *do* that. It's called the

mortal realm.
            Now, about those Saints...this way..."

                        -Steven Shields

Absentee

With truant feet she picked her way
Along the splintered railroad ties.
Her sister trailed not far behind,
Partner in this childish crime.

The engine shrilled a warning blast
And braked, but could not stop
Uncompromising wheels of iron.
Frozen midway on a trestle,
Panicked feet refused to flee
Or leap to river banks below.

Half a school voyeured in shock,
Sat wooden as their aging desks,
Heard whistle drown her whimpering,
Saw homework papers butterfly
A momentary dance of death.

Close to thirty years have passed,
But still my mind reluctantly
Recalls that tragic autumn morn,
And how in life, capriciousness
Can wreck our lives and seal our doom.

-Susan F. Boyter

On the Banks of Sabbath Creek

Sabbath Creek north of Macon
Slow wandering, green and cool
Under pine and sweet persimmon.

Over our ankles we waded
Until we dove and were swimming
In the pool deep and shaded.

My thoughts wild and sprinkled
With laughter. Sunshine dappled
The air blending your freckles

While your smile a scimitar gleam
Sliced into my memory
And the momentary was permanent it seemed

On Sabbath Creek north of Macon
Slow wandering, green and cool
Under pine and sweet persimmon.

I laughed when our hands touched
Helping you up the muddy bank
Hoping love could be this much.

Captive were my thoughts - not yours -
To each new sunrise
Each day bright new colors.

This my hope, our road to follow,
But your future, your plans were otherwise
Said your smile: tender, not callow

On Sabbath Creek north of Macon

Slow wandering, green and cool
Under pine and sweet persimmon.

I dream of your freckles hidden
Behind needles, leaves, and shadows
Wrapped in laughter now forbidden

To enter my thoughts, to enter my heart.
Love had lightly treaded
Now scimitar shimmers and severs apart

On Sabbath Creek north of Macon
Slow wandering, green and cool
Under pine and sweet persimmon.

                                    -T. L. Hensel

Jitterbug Blackbirds and Hula-Popper Sparrows

Clarence only dreamed of lunker lore,
So Mabel marched through menopause in ivy-less
                                    junior college halls,

Crafting poems and trying them out
On her husband's reluctant ears.

Clarence claimed poetry was as foreign to his nature
As dancing a jig -
Didn't even have the words
For either one in his vocabulary.

"Rhyme and litter-action, or whatever -you-callit,
Just idn't my bag.
My mind's on rods and reels, jitterbug blackbirds
And hula-popper sparrows.

"Now you give me a crapshooter,
Or a bayou boogie by Whopper-Stopper,
A shimmy shad from Bass Buster, or a weed eater by
Fleck,
And I can tackle that!

"Let's face it!
When happiness to me is a 14 inch bass,
It's kinda hard to rave over quadruplets –
Or whatever you call those four-line poetry things."

                                    -Susan F. Boyter

65

Radishes

Dirty beads of sweat dotted Red Taylor's forehead. His handkerchief was a damp clump from constant use all afternoon. "And its only May," he thought as he futilely blotted his neck.

"Welcome to Georgia, kid."

His bulk settled in the rusted leaf-spring seat of his 1962 John Deere tractor, Red watched his latest house renter push into a small power mower to cut his grass. Not actually a kid, twenty-two year-old Steve was without his shirt as he mowed the acre lot under a bright May sun that forewarned of a summer that might rival the intense heat of 1968 seven years earlier. Humidity hung heavy, rising from the ground well irrigated after two days of rain. Steve's white sweat band was stained as dark as Red's handkerchief.

He drove his tractor over to the edge of the lawn and worked a cut of Red Man as he waited for the kid to turn off the lawn mower and walk to the tractor.

"Hot day," Red greeted.

"It sure is."

"You going to put in a garden?"

"Garden?" Steve asked as he looked at the grass which was three inches too tall, a handful too thick, and growing in soil bone—jarring rough.

"This back quarter used to be a garden A good garden. Lots of sun and good drainage. I'll come over next week and plow it for you," Red offered.

"Well. Okay."

The next Tuesday, Steve came home from work, got a drink of water at the kitchen sink, looked out the window, and saw that he had a garden plot. Irritated, he walked out to the garden, stood in the center, and kicked a dirt clump. "A lot of work here."

The clean, bright hoe flashed in the sun as stroke after stroke smoothed the garden. As he drove up, Red saw the pile of grass and weeds to the side and was glad the kid had enough sense to glean the trash from the soil. Steve stopped to catch his breath. The strong, almost pungent smell from the freshly cleaved soil was a strange, but pleasant contrast to the clean air riding the May breeze. He liked the pungent smell. It was new to him, and oddly, made him feel like his work in the garden was important. He pushed down with his shoe, leaving an imprint. "This sure seems healthier than that red clay along the road." Just then, Red stepped onto the tilled soil, his old brogans marking his approach with a smooth tread.

"Whatcha going to plant?"

"Some cucumbers, beans, radishes, squash, lettuce, and watermelons."

"It's early for lettuce. Too hot here, fall is the only time you might grow some."

"Tomatoes and cabbage, too. I don't care for cabbage, but Ellen likes slaw, and she's been cooking everything natural since we married."

"Well, you might want to put down some carrots to go into the slaw. Build dirt mounds about this big and start your squash and melons in them"

"Sure."

Squatting, like an Indian, Steve poked four holes in the top of the mound and dropped a squash seed in each. He looked up and surveyed his work. His three squash mounds and speckled pole beans completed one row, then a row of lettuce and cabbage, a row of carrots, and two rows of radishes, white ones, his favorites. "Tomatoes, cucumbers, and some watermelons, and it's finished," he thought as he stood and stretched. Each row was thirty feet long, and behind him was a thirty-foot by thirty-foot plot he just wasn't going to plant.

A bee buzzed by on its way to one of his peach trees still in bloom. He looked across his neighbors' backyards to the woods ringing Smitty's house, then running off across the hill and down to the swamp. "Georgia's a lot like Wisconsin, without the snow in winter," he again thought to himself. He and Ellen had discovered the swamp one Saturday, while tramping through the woods. Marshwiggle Country they called it, after the homeland of Puddleglum, the character in C.S. Lewis's book, *The Silver Chair*. And on the west side of the hill they found Golden Meadow, a quiet, private clearing in the trees that had tall, weedy grass that glowed with golden hues when lit by the sun. They had lain in the meadow and daydreamed. So far, Georgia was a decent place to live.

That night, he and Ellen set lawn chairs next to the garden and talked young couples' talk. When should they have the Chapmans over and what should she serve? When should they head north and meet the rest of his family? When should they begin their family and how many kids?

Time didn't appear to be concrete to those in their twenties.

Steve was on his hands and knees when Red came up and said, "A hoe works good to dig out the weeds."

"Well, weeds look like these baby carrots, and I want to make sure I don't chop them up."

"Your garden's looking pretty good. Did you lay any fertilizer down?"

"No, should I put some down now?"

"Not now, it's too late, but it looks like you won't need it. Steve, you're a hard working man; I'm a member of the Farmers Co-op, and I heard that they are looking for agents. You should talk to them."

"Agents for what?"

"Insurance. It's an insurance co-op for us out here. It'd be a good future."

"No, thanks, I just started this automotive work and I want to stick with it. I've never stuck with anything in my life."

"You're young, and change is easy. You should think about it."

"Too easy, Mr. Taylor. Too easy," Steve thought as he watched the old man walk away and get in his pickup truck. He turned back to his garden, squatted, picked up a dirt clod, and squeezed until it popped and dirt sprayed him and his plants. He looked at the dirt left in his palm, and gently poured it back to the ground.

The flies came with the heat and so did the weeds. He gave up on the empty plot and worked his vegetables. The reedy weeds were knee-high in the vacant space. Some of his watermelon vines were sneaking off into the wild area. He was surprised how everything grew. Baby cukes, little cabbage nodules, tomatoes - good night! And cherry tomatoes! He couldn't figure out where they came from, but he had six plants growing between the rows and at the edge of the wilds. He watered his garden now, and struggled with proper staking design for his tomatoes. They hung out all over the place like teen-agers at a drive-in. His pole beans were easier - one stake, and up they climbed.

It was early July. Steve contentedly planted himself in the chair next to Ellen, alongside the garden.

"Red was right. Look at that lettuce. Not a one grew over two inches. And look at the carrots. There must be something wrong in this soil for them, they're stunted, nothing but runts."

"But Steve, everything else looks beautiful, look how red those tomatoes are. Hey, Red, grab that other chair."

"Ellen. Steve," he acknowledged as he lowered into the chair. "Steve, the garden looks pretty good."

"Yes sir, it grew better than I ever imagined. We even have plenty of cherry tomatoes. I hate cherry tomatoes, but Ellen likes them on salads. And radishes, I counted them yesterday; we've got two hundred seventy white radishes... Ya want some?"

-T. L. Hensel

Recovenanted

I know there must have been jubilation on that forty-first day
When Noah opened the ark to sunlight
After days muffled by clouds and nights of river forging torrents.

Seems like this day is the first I've ever seen the sun,
Felt its life-giving warmth, its fresh-washed illumination.

Holiest of lights draws life up from my toes;
Pulls me to the garden for lauds and bird hymns,
To forage on wet knees for new-sprung weeds,
To gather blossoms crushed by diluvial rains,
To revel in the mystery and the promise.

-Barbara K. Lipe

The Old Ship

Every week day at three O' Clock
   she sits down to hear *The Old Ship of Zion,* and
   I stop playing with my paper dolls,
   slide close to the screen door to watch
   as she puts a Co-cola on the ironing board,
   slides her chair up close to the radio,
   hums, closes her eyes and rocks,
   sometimes waving her hands up
   over her head and sometimes shouting

Oh thank you Jesus! Thank you Jesus! I never know what
   she is so happy about, and I never ask because
   sometimes she cries, her tears mix with snot she
   wipes on her apron and she screams, *What A mighty
   God!*
   especially if they play *Precious Lord.*
   That always makes her cry and she tells me why
   one rainy day when I am inside not playing on the
   porch.
   She says it's the song they sang at George's
   Funeral.
   When her program ends, she is sweaty and tear
   streaked, she makes me lie down for a nap while
   she bathes, combs her hair, puts on a clean print
   dress, ties on a starched white apron, puts on ruby
   lipstick and chestnut face powder on her shiny nose,
   waits on him for dinner,

   the man, not my real granddaddy, just the only one I
   know.

         -Nagueyalti Warren

The Road, A Destination

He never goes the same way twice, never drives the fastest
the most direct, never the straightest route from here to
there. Much better to take back roads through Columbus,
Lumpkin, Cusseta, through Richland, Ellaville,
Westville and Dumas and not arrive in Plains until well
after five.

Much better to tour each town to see if it's alive or dead,
survey home styles, discover a place to eat lunch
or a tourist venue worth a second trip.
Something historical. Something very southern.
Something to do with 'The Great Unpleasantness'
or *Gone With The Wind.*

Anything worth hundreds of pictures on his digital
camera—or me with the wisteria and the crepe myrtle,
or the way kudzu reconfigures the landscape.
Or a disturbing sign—*This is Maddox Country,*
or a funny sign—*Bubba Doo's Famous Hamburgers,*
is surely worth a u-turn or two, worth traveling twice there
and back by the time we get where we're going.

But even after we finally arrive at a motel for the night,
back in the car we go to scout a local place for supper
with mis-typed menu and daily specials like *if its Saturday
its Brunswick Stew for $5.95*
and the waitress calls you honey
and brings your endless refills of sweet tea..

Yes, he's always on the lookout for a memorable place
where we can eavesdrop on the next table
while they yak on about Pappy's pickup,

NASCAR heroes, farming peanuts and yesterday's high school game,
a place with the most remarkable ribs and sweet potato pie,
a place for us to talk about when we finally get home, the long way round.

-Sandy Hokanson

Old Mountain Dreamer

The old red Georgia roads
sparkling with mica dust
fill his heart with dreams
and gold fever.

His hands are numb in the rushing stream
trying to find a nugget, children need shoes.
Tales of a mother lode in California,
his hungry family follows.

Too late, old dreamer, all claims staked out,
No nuggets, no returning home.
The road too rough and long
And no mica dust.

-Rosemary Dixon

An On-Going Conversation

. . . and then there was that night
when the Mad Poet came to town
when we drank that horrible chicory-flavored coffee
and held hands,
and every now and then smiled,
nodding to the rhythm of his words
pretending we understood every nuance,
every metaphor and every simile.

When it came time to leave
we argued, as we always do,
about who would pay the bill,
who would pay the tab,
using poetic gestures
and the little bit of sign language
we learned in that Continuing Education class.

You won, as you always do,
and paid the bill in feminine triumph.
It's funny, I can remember
how your eyes looked
in the street lights
as we walked home
but I can't remember that poet's name.

Was it Bob,
Thomas or
Thunderclap something or the other?
If you know,
if you can recall,
please give me a word, a sign, anything.
I'm tired of sitting here drowning
in the cloying smell of dying flowers
and being afraid to go to bed alone.

-Anderson Frazer

Where a Poem Comes From

The smell of barbecue
drifts from somewhere
across the backyard,
through the screen porch,
in the open door to the den
where the poet sits
trying to write a poem
about love and death,
and suddenly,
on the page,
an arresting image,
unconscious association
of sizzling flesh,
hot fire of passion
and the grill, love
as sauce and pickle
and cole slaw, sliced
white bread; death
as Boston butt, diced,
chipped, served up
in a poem about love, death,
and barbecue, a mediation
on where a poem comes from.

-Ron Self

Lasting Friendship

I reach for the whimsical brown stuffed bear
sitting on my desk,
all dressed up in his green suit, complete with hat.
The seat of the car flashes before me,
like it was only yesterday,
the place you left the bear,
You had never given a gift,
never let me see that side of you.

Lost in New Orleans
we ended up in a Mardi Gras parade.
You watched horrified
as I waved
like Queen Elizabeth
from the Lincoln car window.
Ahh, memories.

I continue to clean the office,
hopeful it will console me.
As I de-clutter,
the bear still reminds me of you.

Oh yes, our unexpected ride
on the railroad tracks
chasing Christmas lights
just "down the road."
The whimsical bear
watched as the headlights
danced in the darkness.

I pause a few moments,
drinking in the all-too-brief time
we were friends

in a world that
devalues true friendship.

I reverently place the bear on the file cabinet,
the memories washing over me
like cleansing rain,
knowing you died much too soon,
your sisterly friendship
still needed to comfort me.

-Brenda P. Dixey

The Poetic Process

One day I heard the Muse. I listened hard
To what she said, and trusting that she knew
A thing or two about what I must do
To earn the nomination of a bard,
I tapped my fluent brain and bled my truant heart
And wrote a poem, then encased it in
An envelope, licked, stamped and placed it in
The mail to see if it might win a part
In some collected works by those like me,
Who turn their truest sentiments to verse,
And send them off with cover letter terse,
So editors will write eventually,
"You're in! You have a 'way with words'!"—a phrase
That means to both my Muse and me high praise.

-Jane Blanchard

Lying Together

Lying together in the dimly-lit room,
I can see your eyes drifting shut as you fade into sleep.
Not yet. Maybe. Not yet.
Your eyes slide half-shut,
then your body jerks as you fight to stay awake,
to make sure that you don't miss a single thing.

You have been fighting sleep for almost a half hour,
thirty long minutes of pacing and rocking and crying
and eye-rubbing and swaying and snuggling.
But now we lie here, looking into each other's eyes.
You stroke my fingers methodically as I use my thumb
to gently pet the back of your chubby little hand.
Stroke, stroke, your delicate skin like silk
under the roughness of my much-chewed thumb.

Your eyes drift ever further, ever further, back in your head,
your eyelids shutting for longer and longer stretches.
At last, sleep has you in his gentle grasp.
I lie with you, watching you breathe,
taking in the sweetness of a face that has done no wrong,
that has known no real hardship,
that is not yet jaded,
as it will be in fifteen years,
if not ten,
if not five.
Quiet as a monk in prayer,
I lift you off of the bed,
snuggling my hand to your face as you start to awaken,
and lay you gently in your crib.
You have put up a valiant fight little knight,
But, for now, the dragon of sleep has won.
That dreaded dragon has won.

-Anna Nero

Where the Rats Live in Piles
An "I remember" poem

I remember that warm summer night driving with
Daddy in his '72 Ford, teal-tinted, rust bleeding through,
my thighs sticking to the vinyl, flip-flops planted firmly on
the floor board that was covered with discarded 8 tracks of
Willie and Waylon and the Boys – and I look into my
Daddy's eyes and smile.

I remember the trash piled in the back; old big
wheels, empty beer cans, a rusty tire taken from the shed
out back, tailgate down, and Daddy driving down the road.
"Can I help sweep it out when we get to the dump?" I
begged. Daddy looked at me with that look like he really
didn't want me to get in the way and said with a sigh, "Just
don't git out the bed of the truck. There's rats in the piles."

I remember the tall pines surrounding us, towering
above on all sides, twilight setting in as Daddy takes the
wrong turn down a dirt road tunnel of eeriness. "Damn! I
need to turn around. I don't think this is the right road."

I remember the sudden low glow of flames
appearing out of the darkness, hooded bodies encircling, a
horse standing erect, cross showing through the flame –
Daddy slams the brakes as I feel his hand pressing against
my head forcing my check against the sweaty vinyl. "Git
down! Stay down! Don't git up! Damn." "What's the
matter?" I ask Daddy through squashed lips. "Are those
men gonna hurt us?"

But most of all I remember Daddy's words –
"Those men don't want us, honey. We got the right color."
When he let me up, we were on the right road to the
dump…where the rats lived in piles.

-Renee Basinger

Oktoberfest

Deep-blue, cloudless October sky,
Curious people line the street.
A parade is ready to pass by,
Soldiers march in step with the beat
Of familiar music, crisp and clear.

In front are the colors, bright and bold,
The red-white-and-blue flying high.
But wait, what is that black-red-and-gold
Banner next to Old Glory?–A cry,
"Can that be a German flag, my dear?"

The column draws nearer at last,
And there, for all to see and know,
The symbols of foes in a distant past
Soar side by side, and proudly show
The war is finally over! I cheer!

So long have I waited for this day,
My heart and mind divided by fate.
It's forty years since that dreadful May,
The land of birth, once safe and great,
Lay beaten in ruins, terror, and fear.

Tears choke my breath as I watch them pass,
The years of secret shame are gone.
The crowd exhibits respect and class,
Humanity's better instincts have won–
And folks return to their pretzels and beer.

-Gerda Tarkington-Smith

Cousin Willy and the Killer Hairbrush

The cousins all loved the first week in July when our parents drove us to Aunt Ida's old two-story white house on Warm Springs Road. We called it Cousins' Week. Our parents called it Freedom Week.

Aunt Ida's house rambled across the foot of a long, downsloping front yard with lines of trees on both sides creating the perfect place for all sort of championship games and fantastic adventures. Behind the house was even better than the front yard with what Mother called a semi-formal garden, a two-story, gray-sided, tin-roofed barn, the chicken coup and a pond. How we loved that pond. It was our ocean; the place where we built and floated pirate rafts to protect the colonies from the king.

The second floor was full of bedrooms and sleeping porches. The windows stayed open all the time in the summer so breezes could cool the house. The rooms had high ceilings and tall windows. Aunt Ida kept the lights off in the daytime convinced this kept the house cooler.

Willy was the oldest and thought he was in charge of us all. I was just a few months younger and it never occurred to him that I really made the decisions. The week before Cousins' Week, one year, I called him and asked, "Willy, have you thought about getting some firecrackers and bringing them to Cousins' Week? You know I can't buy them here in Georgia."

That was all it took. Willy lived on the Alabama side of the Chattahoochee River and firecrackers were legal there.

We decided to test out the firecrackers on Friday afternoon. The Fourth was on Saturday. Willy had hidden the firecrackers in the barn. Nothing was in it but a broken-down tractor. Nobody had farmed the place for years. Aunt Ida taught English at the high school.

I had taken some wooden matches from the kitchen to light the fingerlings. The only firecrackers Willy could get were the little one-inch ones with a fuse, and the brightly-colored poppers you threw down hard to make them explode. I didn't care; it was more than I could get in Columbus.

As we sneaked around the barn to go down to the big rocks on Rainbow Creek, Aunt Ida saw us. She could tell we were up to something. She just didn't know what.

Using her teacher voice, she yelled, "Stop, you two. Come here this instant."

Muttering, "Oh fudge," Willy stuffed the paper bag with the firecrackers into one of his back pockets.

"I know one of you hooligans took my kitchen matches. What are you up to? Setting the pasture on fire like you did last year? Come on, fess up."

We couldn't tell the truth and we couldn't lie. Aunt Ida hated liars. We stood silent.

Pointing at Willy, she said, "You're the oldest so you'll take the lick for both of you."

We pleaded and we begged but we didn't squeal.

She took us into the dim parlor and made us wait while she went to get her hairbrush.

Returning, she sat in her straight-back chair by the window, pointed at Willy and said, "Come here, boy."

Like a man going to the electric chair, Willy walked stifflegged and slowly to her. He knew the routine. He lay across her lap.

She raised the brush and held it high for what seemed like forever.

Then she brought it down, hard. Aunt Ida did not believe in sparing the hairbrush.

Flames...smoke... pops... bangs and screams erupted. I did some of that screaming myself. I saw a shape streaming smoke fly out the window and disappear. I'll never forget Aunt Ida's horrified voice saying, "Oh God, dear God, I've done gone and killed Cousin Willy."

Later we found Cousin Willy soaking his bottom in Rainbow Creek.

Aunt Ida never spanked one of us again.

-Anderson Frazer

Spoons

We have an insatiable yearning to fill ourselves with one another— to scurry inside the other, finding what we want to find.

Obstructed by murky noise and discordant vistas, we escape the hypnotic rituals of distractions like persistent laboratory rats zigzagging their ways through a maze.

God knows the answers, but His wisdom does us little good until we stumble upon it through a million steps and a thousand detours—when we prove to each other and ourselves that there are no exits without unlimited entrances.

I will be happy to show you how I avoided dead-ends and found the best passages, but I can share my journeys only when I realize we never parted in the first place.

Our exits and entrances worm throughout this endless universe, and our arrivals are always ending at our beginnings. Our ends are always dropping as fruit into a basket.

And as soon as I leave, you pass by as one of us slips into a bed somewhere the other cannot find.

I awaken, you sleep. You stir, I doze.

All those miles, all those paths, and we never went anywhere without each other. We never lost ourselves except into each other.

We were never two, except as spoons in a kitchen drawer.

-Don Gerz

Bicycle Breeze

To the top of the hill,
Once and again,
I pedal and push
As hard as I can.

All the while
Picturing me,
Flying low
On a bicycle breeze.

I consider "no hands"
On my way down the hill,
Poised on the margin
Between fear and thrill!

The moments zoom by-
They are fleeting and fine.
I am in charge,
And the world is mine!

Wind is surfing
All around,
As I imagine I'm floating
Over the ground.

No cares or worries,
I'm as free as you please
Because I am one
With a bicycle breeze!

-Lynda Holmes

Third Snow

Then it snowed again,
an amazing unbelievable third snow,
coming down thick, fast, and determined
as if a curtain was being pulled down over the city.
Well, we all obliged. We went home and got off the roads,
huddled up with our families and, like our Georgia
forefathers,
sent out many startled messages about snow.

The sun came up and so did the curtain,
showing off a beaming blue sky
and a city freshly dressed: Atlanta,
dazzling in rolling layers of untouched white,
broad streets bare as summer shoulders,
multiple skylines catching the light
and throwing it back.

It was a celebration, the third snow
in a land of little winter.
We put on our coats and went out to dance.

Underneath Magnolias

Underneath magnolias
Ice is slow to melt.
That stubborn southern tree hoards
The spit of winter
Til the tulips start their shouting.
Underneath magnolias
The right kind of child
Can have a mansion:
A kitchen, a door,
A stable for a difficult horse.

Underneath magnolias
Grudges won't die.
There's too much room under the crown
Too much beauty in the blossom
To cut it down.
It's a bully, the grandiflora,
See how the house behind it
Hides from the street.

Spring Gossip

The gossip starts with
the daffodils—
early, pretty, beloved.
The irises can't abide them,
spread lies to the sky.
Oaks just beginning to green
blush beards of embarrassment.
Later, the grass throws a get-together.
Everyone stands around in clumps
swaying to the music.
The azaleas get mad,
raise a racket of pink and white.
The whole yard laughs.
Even the dogwood shows its fragile smile.

-Hilary King

Homonyms Synonyms and Momma 'nems

My Momma 'nem
Used to say
"Ya'll light and come in."
Maybe your Momma 'nem said,
"Set a spell."
Country folk talked different
But they meant well.

My Momma 'nem
Worked in a cotton field.
Maybe your momma 'nem worked
In a cotton mill.
But come Sunday or Sabbath,
It was wear white,
And come clean.

Now Preacher 'nem
Didn't care too much
For homonyms
Or synonyms,
It was all sin
To him.
He'd say,
Whether you're just mean
Or you mean well,
If you sin
You're going to hell.
And that went for
Momma 'nem,
Daddy 'nem,
President 'nem
Aunt Cora 'nem…….

-Freddie O'Connor Riley

Got This at Goodwill

Bins full-
The thrown away
This don't play
Couldn't sell this for pay
Didn't want this anyway
Plain old everyday
Has beens.

I went out of style
Tried on
Somebody's old shoes
And walked a mile
Found a good old tune
On a dial
Not on a file
Held up
A raggedy
any doll
to a little girl
watched her smile

Some folks still believe
That it is more blessed to give
Than to receive
Life is full of blessings
Salvaged
From yesterday.
Good morning,
Welcome to goodwill.

-Freddie O'Connor Riley

About the Author

The poet looks sincerely troubled
despite the light behind her, sun
signaling to Earth,
>   *All is well.*
Something blooms in the background,
something purplish that reminds one
of bougainvillea, but what?

A botanist could tell, perhaps, or the poet,
if she remembers the fineness of the day
and what it was that ordered sadness,
anger by its side, to climb into her eyes—
and not, as one would hope, hope itself—
moments before the camera blinked.

In My Psalm

David is a shepherd still
and is content to eat his bread
and talk to stars and sheep
until his unanointed head rests
on the dust and his hair
and the brush grow into each other.
He greets the sun with a loud whoop
and dances in circles so small
that he dizzies and falls and laughs
his belly into hurting,
and no one rebukes him because
no one sees. This David is alone
on the ocean of the wild;
anything can happen (and he wishes
it will)—a lion awake, for instance,
after dreaming of eating a man's heart.

This David never leaves the wind's side,
and he loves lightning
but no better than thunder,
and if anyone tried to make him a king
he would feign madness, wander further
into nothingness, ask El Shaddai
to strike him blind should he ever lose sight
of the mountains or a single lamb
trying to stand on wobbly legs.

-Jacob Martin

Memoir

Remembering isn't necessarily easy.
Exactly what did happen?
With whom?
And when?
Not to mention where?
Since recollection comes in bits and pieces,
A record of a lifetime is a mere collage,
A scrapbook cluttered with cards
And tickets and pictures,
A mosaic of shards and slivers
Distorting the image in the mirror.
How does one arrange the fragments of the past
In order to represent the truth of
What was, what is, and what will be?
Remembering isn't necessarily easy.
But neither is forgetting.

-Jane Blanchard

Daddy's Brain

Daddy's brain floats in a fancy glass jar on our living room mantle. Mama had the doctors put his brain in the jar after Daddy fell down the stairs. She says the real him is still inside his brain.

Granny Annie tells me that even though Daddy can't touch us any more, he knows every thing that happens in the living room. I don't know how he does that. When Uncle Tommy comes home from the Navy, I'm going to ask him to tell me how Daddy does that.

Any time I go into the living room where Daddy's brain lives, I get nervous. I try to be quiet so he will not notice me. Sometimes I take off my shoes and tiptoe. When I do and Granny Annie sees me, she says, "Boy, quit being so skittish. Your daddy can't hurt you anymore. Your Mama took care of that."

Mama likes to sit on the sofa in the living room with her new friend Jerry. Jerry is a girl and her real name is Geraldine. I think Jerry is neat. She tells me how smart I am and says I will grow up to be an astronaut just like her. I hope she's right.

When Mama and Jerry sit on the sofa holding hands and talking, the green water in Daddy's jar begins to bubble. If they keep talking and having a good time, the bubbles get so thick you can't see his brain at all.

I don't know why Mama keeps Daddy's brain on the mantel. He was mean to all of us when his brain lived in his head.

-Anderson Frazer

The First Glimpse

Alone in the emergency room of St. Mary's hospital, I face my biggest fear. I have been here for hours, lying on my right side, legs pulled up to my chest, the only position that makes me anywhere close to comfortable, even after the shot of Comprazine I got in my hip over an hour ago. Even this is preferable to lying on my roommate's bed because I can't get into my loft, being declared "Poor little lump" by Tennille before she goes to study at the library, better than having my belly probed, which makes me defy gravity, my upper body coming right up off the table. I blame it all on Huddle House, the sickness I feel, and I know Mom and Dad are on their way, which should be a comfort.

For now I lie in wait, bathed in the dim glow of florescent lighting, arm aching from fluids pushed through the IV, the room chilly and reeking of sterility. Hours before, I finally gave in and called my Mom, told her how I was feeling. She sighed, "Well, go on up to St. Mary's and give me a call when they tell you something." I went to the hospital, which was right up the street from Brumby, my dorm, affectionately referred to as the "Virgin Vault" because of its visitation policy, and checked myself into the ER. Mom called and was transferred to my room, and she and Dad headed toward Athens from Washington minutes later.

Now, one thing my parents don't know about me is that I have a tattoo, a tribal band around the upper part of my left arm, my eighteenth birthday present to myself. Somehow I have managed to hide it for almost a whole year, and it's looking like my cover will be blown. As you may or may not know, you can't really hide ANYTHING in a hospital gown. I tell a nurse about my situation, and she is sympathetic. "Here," she says, handing me a second hospital gown, this one with long sleeves. "You can wear this like a robe." I am very grateful, the almost transparent cotton camouflaging the ink *just* enough to keep me safe from the wrath of my mother.

Minutes after Mom and Dad find me in the ER, the surgeon comes in for the consult. He says, "The difficulty here is that we can't tell how you *really* feel because you've gotten the shot of Comprazine. We can wait until morning when you *really* feel good or we can go ahead and do the surgery and, worst case scenario, we take out a healthy appendix." We decide to go ahead and do the surgery that night.

This is it, the jig is up. I know that if I am going into surgery, my "robe" is coming off. The minute my mother sees that tattoo, she puffs up in anger. "What is that!?! What is that?!?! YOU SHOW YOUR FATHER!!!" In a way, I totally expected this reaction, but I still can't believe it. Here I am, in pain, terrified, about to go into surgery, and she is angry about a tattoo. Later Dad would tell me that he actually thought it was pretty cool, but he dares not say that out loud in front of my raging *madre*. I am wheeled into pre-op, where a man in penguin scrubs begins prepping me for surgery. The smell of cleaning agents burns my nose a little, reminding me of the day I went to Midnight Iguana Tattoo in Athens, sat in the vinyl seat, feeling the sting of the needle marking me as an adult.

The surgery goes well, recovery is relatively uneventful. It turns out that if they had waited until morning, my appendix would have ruptured. The nurses want me to hug a pillow and cough, and that is the last thing I want to do, but they say they I have to rid myself of the remnants of anesthesia. The next day, I am released to my parents with orders to take it easy. I get a ticket outside the dorm for parking in a fire lane when I go to pick up some clothes to take for my week of recovery.

The tattoo is not much of an issue after that, though after I get my cartilage pierced, she screams at me "NO MORE! If you don't like your body, that doesn't mean you have to desecrate it!" Two tattoos later, it's not really a big deal, though she sometimes says that eventually I'll be looking to have them removed, which is highly unlikely. I'm not sure if she has lightened up or given up. Or maybe she has determined that body modification is not a one-way path to failure or skeeziness.

Now that I have a fourth one, I know nothing will compare to her reaction to the first glimpse of that band of ink, the defiant act that symbolized for me my separation from my family, my passage into adulthood. None of the other symbols of my coming of age were nearly as easy as sitting in that chair, listening to the buzz, enraptured by the sting of growing up. I hope she understands that now.

-Anna Nero

Firestorm

Flashing
Flames of fury
Red, orange, yellow
Incandescent
The inferno forages
Insatiable…
Splaying, streaking, sprawling, swooping, sweeping
Rambling, roaring, rustling, reaching
Roasting…
Sparking straw, singeing soil
Igniting lightwood
Tenderizing tough timber
Parching the landscape,
Baking branches brittle,
Sizzling seedlings, sautéing shoots, scorching stems,
Incinerating deadwood,
Petrifying stout trees, charring the bark skin
Seeking sustenance
Slicing through tangy wood,
Tearing through thickets
Gutting the forest
Feasting…
Crunching spiny cones grazing strewn straw munching
coarse
mulch biting blackened bark gnashing hefty limbs gulping
seasoned sticks savoring gnarled vines licking loose leaves,
nibbling frizzled foliage consuming crisp twigs gobbling
hardy
brush gnawing tall timber chomping brawny boughs
devouring
sinewy saplings
glutting atrophied tree trunks
Bingeing…

Belching acrid heat
A toxic wind roils
Billowing thick, pungent smoke
Surging, sweltering, strangling, smothering

Churning, choking...
Out-of-control, the demon wildfire gorges,
Reducing arid forest to cinder
In a mindless,
Fiery onslaught.

-Mary A. Gervin

Fire Ants

Fast, furious, frantic
Invaded troopers rally.
Roused from their trenches,
Embattled insects surge.
Antennae twitching,
The noxious horde advances,
Tiny tenacious warriors
Inflicting sting after sting.

-Mary A. Gervin

Adrenalin Junkie

Thrashing and tumbling headlong,
A skydiver
Rushes into the abyss
Impugning fear
Lolling amid wispy clouds,
Languid limbs levitating.
Spread eagled, the daredevil wafts
—Kitelike—
Enthralled in ephemeral rapture
Engaging the ripcord
—Kite on the wing a feint—
Earthbound again
Restless
Reckless

-Mary A. Gervin

A Breeze

For a moment a caressing breeze
cools the heavy heat,
and grace returns.

Like leaves swirling round and round
on the clear waters of a mountain creek,
memories ride the waving breeze.

For a moment, memories return upstream,
back to the spring of our beginning,
to the grand hopes we once were,
to the hopes we do remember
in the winter of our lives.

-Mario R. Mion

The Layover

Springtime in Berlin, 1944. The world was in combat, and the war was going badly for Germany. Still, there were sunfilled days when I could almost forget the nearly constant bombing raids that ravished our city. I was 15, and my youthful optimism battled with the ever-present fear for my brother on the Russian front. My ailing mother was my other ever-aching concern. But in the five long years since the war began I had learned to cope with misery, hunger, cold, deprivations, and death raining from the sky. We children went to school; we played our games and grew up in spite of everything, always hoping to survive one more day.

Since I lived close to the zoo and had always been an animal nut, I was a frequent visitor to this oasis that had been so far spared destruction. I knew most of the inhabitants as personal friends and often brought them potato peels and other kitchen garbage, as well as acorns, chestnuts, and walnuts. Feeding the animals was not only allowed in those days but encouraged wholeheartedly because the animals' rations were slim, too.

This day, I suddenly had a companion. A very young soldier was by my side as I watched the seals getting their midday feeding, and soon we were talking. Being a student at an allgirl school I felt awkward around males, but I became more comfortable as we walked on. The young man beside me was handsome with a boyish face and a deep tan. He told me his name was Stefan, and his outfit was on the way to the Eastern Front. His train had a two-hour layover, and he had come to spend that time in more pleasant surroundings than the noisy railroad station adjacent to the zoo. So here we were, enjoying the warm, sunny afternoon in unexpected company.

When it was time to return to the station, he asked me to accompany him. Would I, please? I knew I would be late getting home, and Mama would ask all kinds of questions, but I agreed. I would think of something to tell Mama. Once there, he asked me for my address, and would I send a picture as soon as possible? He looked so anxious and had such a winning smile, I promised to write as soon as he was able to send his address from the front. And then it was time to board the train. He looked at me pleadingly and asked me to kiss him good-bye!

I suddenly panicked. Oh no, I couldn't couldn't do that! I had never kissed a man before, and besides, what would people say? He laughed and convinced me that kissing at railroad stations was practically obligatory. So, I summoned all my courage and gave him a quick peck on the lips. He jumped on the train as it started to roll, waved like mad, and admonished me to write him, one last time. I waved back and watched the train disappear.

When I got home, Mama was her most inquisitive self. She demanded to know my whereabouts since school, just as I predicted. I tried evasion, but I was a poor liar. I never could keep secrets from my mother somehow. Mama had a way of looking straight into my innermost. She used to tell me that she could tell by my nose if I told fibs. Deep down, I was still half convinced that this was true. I went to bed with a bad conscience, feeling sure that the truth would come out. Someone might have seen me kissing that young soldier and tell. Grown-ups always stuck together.

I thought about the kiss, how awkward and shy I had felt, but how sweet it had been, my first real kiss. Stefan was handsome and fun to talk to, and I hoped he would keep his promise to write. And I cherished my little secret, for a few days, anyway.

The following week, I raided the mailbox every day

the minute I came home from school. Mama became very curious because I had never shown such interest in what the postman brought, unless it was a letter from my brother Rudi whose letters from Russia were rather infrequent. Maybe it was too soon to expect mail from so far away.

It became more difficult each day to hide my disappointment while Mama watched me ever more closely, and I finally confessed and told her all about that afternoon at the zoo. I had anticipated Mama's alarm—her little girl and a soldier? After all, I was still a complete child. Frantically, I tried to allay her fears and pleaded with her to let me know when the letter arrived. I promised to let her read it, and all. Stefan is such a nice boy. . . I ran on and on.

Mama was looking out of the window and did not answer. I had expected a lecture, but her mood was pensive. There was a strange look on her face, a mixture of love and pain and resignation in her eyes. For a second I thought I saw something else. Could it be guilt? Impossible! I dismissed the rising suspicion immediately. Mama wouldn't. She loved me, I knew that beyond a doubt. She couldn't do anything that would hurt me.

As I kept looking for that letter, I began to feel awful and foolish. Why had Stefan wanted my address? Had something happened to him? Was he just playing a game? After weeks of searching the mail fruitlessly, I became frantic. And, as always in a crisis, I turned to my big brother. I wrote him all about Stefan, desperately needing some reassurance. Rudi wrote back, and in his inimitable, blunt but gentle way straightened out my befuddled head.

He wrote that while I shouldn't give up hope, I should realize that I was awfully young and inexperienced, and that some men, especially soldiers, sometimes collect pictures from girls and then tell all kinds of stories about

101

them, not all of them complimentary. And he didn't want his little sister's photo in a lot of soldiers' wallets so they could brag about her.

In fact, Rudi did what Mama had failed to do so far–he explained the facts of life to his little sister who was in dire need of them. In addition, he admonished me to always believe Mama before trusting a stranger, since I could be sure that Mama had my best interest at heart and would never hurt me, as a stranger might.

During the days that followed I clung to every word in Rudi's letter. I trusted him implicitly, and when I finally stopped looking for mail, I put the episode out of my mind and concentrated on school again. Schoolwork had suffered considerably, for the first time in my life. Things went back to normal at last, and I went back to being a kid. At the time I didn't know just how crucial my brother's words were, but they probably kept me from making some serious blunders. That letter was one of the last he ever wrote. It gave me the layover I required, time to grow up patiently.

Not until much later, long after Mama's death, did I find out from Aunt Sophie what had really happened. Mama had intercepted Stefan's letter, read it, and destroyed it in a wave of anxiety. Her little girl and a man? In these uncertain times? As young as she is? When we had our talk it was already too late, and Mama couldn't bring herself to justify her haste.

I did not hold it against her, but not until I had a daughter of my own did I fully appreciate what motivated her to commit this breach of trust. Still, I somehow wish Aunt Sophie had kept Mama's secret, and I can't help wondering what Stefan thought about the girl who never wrote back.

I never saw him again.

                                        -Gerda Tarkington-Smith

102

Meditations on a Flame

How does it, simple being, burn and keep burning
in a temple as wrought, as encompassing as night?

It seems to support the weight of darkness, the great dome
above, in which a dream must find a fissure
so it may fly.

It grows as though called upon by far-off suns.

Itself a small sun, it is now the center of my small system,
an almost-empty circle.

My pen pushes on a line only because this star has fallen
into the candle's crater.

What was it the Creator said? Was it, *Let there be light,*
or was it, *Let what light there is, be?*

We make what we can by what light there is.

What light: enough to sate my two famished eyes.

How it clings like a bird to a branch, holds on before the
breath,
the wind of my lungs blowing, forcing it to shudder, shy
away.

It is the lone flower in the garden, coming out of nothing,
folding into nothing.

-Jacob Martin

Oh, What a Day

A pony tail blonde in a black Sebring convertible
rules the universe on a day like this.
Spring promises to come to your bed
like the lush maiden of summer.
Turkey season doesn't usually begin like this.
Where are the winds screeching through the pines
like untrimmed fingernails on a blackboard?
The thermometer on a rusted coathanger
reads 40 degrees. Mild compared with other years.
Sunrise usually glares in your eyes
like silver shined for the preacher
coming to Sunday dinner.
Today, the first rays are like the old gold
on grandfather's pocket watch.
Mosquitoes, redbugs, and ticks haven't reset their clocks
to Daylight Savings Time.
Pollen hasn't coated the woods with lime dust.
Gobbling toms have forgotten the lead pellets
which swarmed at them like enraged killer bees.
A day like this is gravid with hope. All things seem
possible.
For a wing-footed moment, I don't limp on a bad knee,
and forget the pain which shot up my back like lightning
when my feet swung off the cot.
I can ignore my new pill box,
the one with larger compartments.
Who knows, on a day like this,
the blonde in the Sebring
might even look twice.

-John Ottley, Jr.

Get God in Your Game

The men's Bible class wanted
to get God with them on the golf course.
I offered that I shout His name
after every shot.
Sober faces around the circle.
That wasn't exactly what they meant.

I have narrowed to 300 the things I think about
when starting my backswing.
Should God be #301?

The leader said we should trust God
the way we trust our golf swing.
I could do that, but, frankly, it's a downer
when I slice a Titelist Pro-V1 high and wide
into impenetrable kudzu and poison ivy.
We'd like to think the Lord has better control.

These virtuous men:
fellows, really, it's OK
to spend Sunday on the links.

-John Ottley, Jr.

December in Atlanta

In the great snowfall of my imagination—wet, a bit, and blue
as skim milk on bare, black branches twisting skyward

like the fingers of old women--the city, transformed in its winter
coat, sees its icons anew: at the Big Chicken, only its red,

disembodied head peeps through the drifts, though the scent
of wings and breasts, salty and fat, permeates the air.

On Grant Field, Yellow Jackets make hump-backed
snow-angels in their football uniforms, while windows

in Midtown glitter like ice caves behind them. Peachtree,
usually clogged as winter noses, is empty of traffic,

and the lights of the Fox lose their garishness as their glow
puddles in the street in perfect circles. Meanwhile, the animals

of the Zoo hunker down in their habitats, while the elephants
and gorillas, used to an Atlantan approximation of Africa,

marvel at what falls; to the east, Stone Mountain rises up
like the snowball to end all fights. All of this makes residents

playful; they might even sled, if they could, down the tongue-twisting
slopes of Spaghetti Junction, that gnarl of interstates,

never breaking, never cursing the person ahead, gliding faster
toward 285 than they ever have in a car on a Friday afternoon.

Or maybe they'd skate in the Fountain of Rings in Centennial Park,
the water from the run-off of the cascades frozen to a thick sheet

of ice even the Thrashers would approve of. For a day or so would come happiness, but they'd tire soon of the temperature,

wish again for the sun to burn the frost off their bones, putting winter behind them as if it never happened.

-JC Reilly

Late Summer Music

As I lie in the old Hatteras hammock,
four sets of chimes jangle in the pecan
trees, less from the wind as the trio
of squirrels that soar from limb to limb

like acrobats. The wood is soft,
and under even their slight weight,
some small branches bend too far, snap
as the squirrels reach the next bough.

Still green in their husks, clustered
nuts on twigs plummet to the ground,
while the squirrels chuff and chitter
in annoyance, or at least some chatter

that sounds as though they are talking over
each other like family at a holiday feast.
They do not head for the easy, fallen
pecans as I think they might, though one

deserts its perch on a thicker limb to race
around the trunk of the tree and the others
give chase, claws scritch-scratch-scraping
the bark as they zip like Loony Toons,

so quickly I wonder how they don't
get dizzy, as I almost do, watching them.
When the squirrels spiral to the base
of the trunk and skitter out of the yard,

the chimes no longer clang against each
other, and gentler notes lift from the leaves
as the wind now remembers its task,
the afternoon's concert subdued, sweet as sighs.

-JC Reilly

5Ever

Someone's grayed out the Valentine on the R. J. Griffin
sign: *I love you 5ever* now smoky clouds of paint.
Mornings on the commute into work, I'd drive past
the corner of the construction site where it stands,
imagine who sprayed that sweet communiqué—

your Great Lover, perhaps—part-Romeo, part-Ninja,
part-Basquiat, who sneaked downtown one night,
Krylon in hand, slipped past thugs and addicts,
dodged zealous watchmen, to leave this promise to you:
that his love, too, builds here, the eternity of *5ever*

limitless as the stories of any hi-rise. Your sweetheart,
who spurned paper as too flimsy a surface to blazon
bold vows, craved instead the durability, the visibility
of public signage—but was thrifty enough not to rent
a billboard of his own (the better to save money

to lavish you with baubles and sparkles and silks).
I hoped you thanked him, and kissed him—as I would,
were he mine. So now when I see the blighted sign
that scars my romance-riddled heart, I wonder
what bitterness Griffin bore to deface those words of love,

this Griffin so unlike its folklore namesake known
for guarding the priceless, mating for life, never to seek
a new mate should the first die. *That* griffin loved
always, as your paramour promises to love you. But oh,
the impermanence of language—forever is not always
enough.

-JC Reilly

109

The Gig

Lights, camera, satisfaction!
Tickets shuffling, crowds roaring
People, popcorn, possibility.

Fans staring, music booming
Stomp, clap, groove
Artist creating, beat is painting.

Wind, wonder, whip
Knees knocking, Brown not talking
Soul, inspire, hit.

Atmosphere jiving, vocals uniting
Rhythm, rocking, radiant.

Longing to say, lacking the form
Journey, experience, effort?

Connecting the notes, birthing a tune
Construct, content, control.

-Steven Dunn

Fallen

Away from grace, away from love.
Wanting to be in the sky above.
Away from trouble, away from twist.

Longing for nature's soft blissful kiss.
Not sure where to go.
Or even if there's a tomorrow.

Lost in the vines.
Tangled, broken, and weak.
No longer divine.

Whose suppose to be meek?
Gasping for air, from the true wind of life.
Begging for water, when there's none in sight.

Where to start or where to end.
Needing the directions, just to begin.
Frozen in time, not moving an inch.
Clear to see it always happens again.

-Steven Dunn

Legacy
The tottering stone cairns of my ancestors
Stretch in mute, mossy rows beneath the cedars,
Their weathered headstones
Bearing terse messages of birth and death.
Ancient unseen eyes observe
From under the cold clay
As I prowl curiously among the mounds,
Scribbling dates, bloodlines, epitaphs.
A strong sense of family pervades the place;
Grey-clad Confederates and kilted kinsmen mingle there
In a mélange of the dusty past.
At day's end the sun draws his tattered twilight robe
Around the waning warmth.
The moon rises warily through the black boughs
To hang her shining silver coin
Above the scene.
Shivering in the chill,
I note the grassy space where I will lie
When mortality fails.

-Judy F. Brouillette

Yard Sale after the Funeral

On the sun-dappled lawn, three aging sisters sat
Becalmed in ancient chairs,
Like lizards on a sunny rock,
Reflecting on their past.

The chipped and faded cups they held
Evoked early mornings at the silent table,
The clink of forks and crunch of toast
The only discourse among disparate souls.
Of the antique clock of gilded cupids
Embracing its shattered crystal
The eldest eternally cried,"Why buy them when they're
cracked?"
Her mother pursed tight lips
And folded cracks and all within possessive arms.
"They're old," she said, and
None disparaged logic such as hers.

The timeworn mixer whirred through myriad cakes
And whisked potatoes to a snowy mound
For every Sunday dinner.
But through it all, the thread of Father's censure ran,
"The gravy's salty, the meat too done,
The bread's not thin like my mother made."
His diatribe made pieces of the meal
Stick in unexpected places.

The silence on the lawn recalls
Those days before their hearts converged,
Three vines clinging to a common tree;
But now they, too, are old.
Is age the only gauge of worth?
The broken veins and withered skin

Bespeak a kingly portion.
Who values these when Mother now is gone?

-Judy F. Brouillette

Déjà Vu

The blank, rusty eyes at the railroad crossing
Stare past the rotting trestle
To the rank patch of peppergrass and bitterweed.
The cracked lenses no longer signal red and green,
For the train will never pass this way again.
The wide concrete platforms of the old depot,
Once stacked with cracked valises and alligator bags,
Have become a smooth rink
Where skittering brown leaves skate before the wind.

The heavy oak door moves at my touch
With a surly, rasping creak,
And the dusty waiting room echoes my footsteps.
High above, the ceiling of narrow boards
Drops flakes of depot green on festoons of fluttering
cobwebs.
A breath of moldy past assails my senses:
Early childhood travels on a coal-burning train;
Scratchy horsehair seats and tepid drinking water;
Soot from the stack pouring through open windows;
And even after nearly sixty years,
The whistle's lonely wail
Still sounds within my mind.

-Judy F. Brouillette

Possibilities

As a child playing in the Chicago suburbs, Farah's father had said of his eldest daughter that she was as nimble as the ibex, always finding her feet. Farah, not knowing what the ibex was, had looked it up in the fat encyclopedia in the school's library, and then been proud of the comparison. The ibex was a survivor, living on nearly sheer cliffs and finding foot holds in the smallest of spaces.

Her younger sister, Lina, their father said, was as fleet of foot as the gazelle. Farah was instantly jealous; impressive the ibex might have been, but the gazelle had always been equated with beauty.

Years later, because she had the surefootedness of the ibex and her mother's magical heritage, Farah knew she had not simply stumbled on the trail to the top of Stone Mountain. Her jinn heritage and training allowed her to feel the blip of magic that caused her misstep. Farah Osman did not stumble or lose her footing

Farah opened her senses, settled into the core of her being, and let her perception play out across the trail, her consciousness flitting from person to person as she walked.

There.

Behind her, she felt the tick of another of mixed heritage. He felt much like her half jinn, half human mother—considerably stronger than she or her sister, who were only one quarter jinn.

Farah turned around to look down the trail at the one who'd tripped her. She saw a tall man—he stood well over most everyone near him—wearing faded jeans, ragged Chucks, and a worn Georgia Tech hoodie. He had an older 35mm SLR in his hands, and the neck strap dangled loose. She tried to figure out what he had slung across his back, which had a strap that stretched from his right shoulder to the opposite hip, but stopped when he smiled up at her and winked. She smirked back.

Waiting as he slowly made his way up the trail to her was annoying, but she certainly wasn't going to backtrack. She hunched into her navy sweatshirt, gold "EMORY" emblazoned across the front, as a gust of wind cut through the dense fabric. Farah was glad for the impulse in the parking lot that had led to her pulling it out of her car's back seat. She hadn't realized how much the temperature dipped as the elevation increased.

When he finally reached her, he stood taller than she, though he was standing somewhat below her on the trail. Farah was six feet; she didn't usually look up at anyone. It had been obvious before that he was tall, but having him close, it was shocking. This close, too, she realized he was very attractive. With his fair skin, dark hair, and expressive eyes, he was the definition of handsome. And he appeared, of course, when she was looking not her best.

"Numair," he said, moving the camera to his left hand and offering her his right.

She nodded as she took his hand. "Numair," she said, "I'm Farah. How nice to be tripped by you."

Rather than shaking her hand, as she expected, he brought it to his lips, which he brushed against her knuckles. The huge smile on his face as he did this had her internally rolling her eyes. The man had no shame. He gave her hand a brief squeeze before releasing it.

"I've never tripped someone so beautiful before," he said, his smile still ridiculously large, "I wasn't sure it would work."

Making a face at him, Farah turned and started back up the trail. With Numair parallel to her, she saw it was a tripod strung across his back; the strap attached to it looked as though it had been hastily rigged. She wondered why he hadn't used his magic to conjure a carrying bag. Even she, with her limited power, could have managed it, and this close she could tell he was more than powerful enough. "Try to trip me again," she said, pretending she could take him on and win, "and I'll bump you off the mountain."

Numair laughed, and she found herself delighted. "If I tripped you again, beautiful lady, I would deserve it."

They walked in silence for a time, and Farah was glad to know that he understood the value of a quiet moment. His ability to just *be* recommended him far more than his looks or child-like method of catching her attention. She found herself frequently looking his way as they walked, and caught him as he glanced at her.

Soon they found themselves at a spot on the trail that was rougher and pocked with water-filled indentions. Numair offered his hand to her, a gesture meant to help her on the uneven terrain, she knew. Rather than taking it, she bounced ahead several feet, her balance perfect, her confidence absolute. She turned on a nobby ridge of stone to face him, letting him get a bit closer, then matched his pace, walking backward up the trail, her faith in her ability unwavering.

"My father," she told him as they walked, she backwards, he forwards with a wary—but amazed— expression on his face, "said as I grew up that I reminded him of the ibex of Central Asia, always staying on my feet, never missing my footing." She felt her face soften as she thought about her father. It had been a few weeks since she'd called her parents, so she promised herself she'd pick up the phone when she got back to the dorm.

"Your father is an astute man." Numair's expression was admiring. "You have their tenaciousness, their nimbleness, as well as the gazelle's beauty."

She opened her mouth to argue with him, to tell him it was her sister who was the beauty, but he continued as though he wasn't looking right at her, couldn't tell she wanted to talk.

"I have seen both, Farah. I spent two years with my father's people in Damascus and Beirut, and traveled all over the region. There is nothing you can say that would convince me that you do not have the best aspects of both animals."

Farah stopped abruptly, stunned that this man could so completely win her over. They'd met less than an hour ago.

This time when he caught up to her, it was not the mischievous smile she saw, but a softer, more sincere one. Numair reached up and brushed a dark, errant lock of hair from her forehead. Internally, she both swooned at the action and winced at how her frizzy cloud of hair was of course working its way out of the hair tie. By his expression, though, whatever he was seeing wasn't the too-tall, plain girl she saw when she washed her face each evening. Her stomach twisted nervously, and she wasn't sure how to react. What did you do when a handsome jinni flirted so outrageously, and made you feel beautiful even when you knew you weren't?

If you were Farah, you would blurt out what your mother always said when you had been particularly frustrating: as surefooted as the ibex, perhaps, but most definitely sharing its other trait. "Stubborn."

He tilted his head, visibly considering her apparent *non sequitur*. His right eyebrow rose in silent question.

"My mother," she said, "would add that to the traits I share with the ibex. As stubborn as a goat who insists rocky crags and dangerous cliffs are a good place to live."

His laugh was deep and thick with amusement. "My father equated me to a donkey. Nothing so poetic as a nimble goat, determined to outwit predators. Just a lowly

117

beast of burden digging in its heels rather than be told what to do."

Farah chuckled. "Are you sure we're not related?"

He shook his head. "I think we're safe. We only share a few traits." Numair gestured behind her. "We've nearly reached the top."

They finished the trail in a silence that felt happy. The mirth and good mood she felt was also radiating off of her companion. They worked their way across the top of the mountain, close to a fence that ringed the perimeter. Turning slowly, she could see the Atlanta suburbs, and Atlanta itself, spread out at her feet. The trees below were a mix of green and the beginnings of autumn's yellows, reds, and oranges. Her breath caught, and her magic escaped her for a moment, a shimmering strand of sparks dancing along the chain link fence before them.

"Look at that," he said softly. "The world laid out in all its possibilities." She felt him wrap his arm around her shoulders, and though she hadn't known him long, she let him, and allowed him to pull her close, so that she was pressed against his side.

Farah looked up and caught his eye. "Do you feel them," she asked, "the possibilities?"

He squeezed her shoulder. "I do," he said quietly, "I do."

-Jessica Nasca

the garden

when my good friend inquires of me
how a garden becomes perfect
and asks because she *wants* to know
is it the peacocks that greet flannery
or the jasmine perfume at night
could it be the honeysuckle
with sweet treats waiting for the tongue
to touch;

and impulsive rosemary
crushed between fingers?

perhaps a
bench under wisteria and
bulbed tulips, crocus, hyacinths
with waxy gardenias that sweetly
scent the cooling deep dusk
so i answer my friend's query
how a garden becomes perfect
are those things invited to stay
to embed themselves and become
comfortable—from the angel
to the mossy birdbath—
to you

-Kathleen McKenzie

Bridges

Bridges are platforms of support enabling you to cross over obstacles in your path. Most bridges in my life were not made of steel and concrete. They were comprised of flesh and blood and lots of love.

My first bridge was my grandmother. She taught me discipline and responsibility while giving me a soft lap to crawl into after a fall.

My next bridge was a fourth grade teacher that arranged for me to go to a speech school. She saw a bright child behind the gibberish of my speech. This one act of support helped how I communicated to the world, as well as how I was viewed. Today I probably would get stuck in Special Ed classes simply because no one could understand my words.

My high school Dean of Girls was my bridge to accomplishment with one sentence. One day, Miss Tramell hauled a group of lazy students (including me) into the auditorium and expressed her disappointment in us – all of us capable of "A" work – none of us achieving it. From that day forward, I put my best efforts into school and reaped the rewards of knowing I was doing my best.

To afford college, I worked in an old general store called P.I. Richardson's general Store. The 'poor' John Richardson (his cousin John was the rich one – he joked) scheduled my work hours around my classes. His teachings may have been more valuable than any of my college classes.

Early on, he told me to remember our customers' names. He said everyone feels good when they are remembered.

By greeting them by name, it perked them up and hopefully ready to buy more. I have carried that habit into my life, always making an effort to remember people's names.

The bridge of college would have been too high without family members: my brother-in-law Woodrow furnishing a ride whenever needed, Daddy giving me lunch money like I was still in elementary school, and Mother babysitting Amanda during my second stint of college after my divorce.

When I think of bridges, I see Amanda's arms, as a tiny child reaching up for a lift into my arms, needing me. She taught me the pains and joys of taking care of someone, helping them over the bridges of their life.

Sometimes bridges are long and hard to cross: tending to an elderly aunt with Alzheimer's brought tears of exasperation and peals of laughter, reading poetry all day until a dear friend takes her last breath, watching parents and brothers cross their last bridges, wondering where your next bridge will lead.

-Lavonda Forbes

Traveling through Georgia

The summer I turned twelve my brother and I took our first trip south from Tennessee through Georgia to Florida. Today, a divorced daughter of a moderately bipolar mother and an alcoholic father, I would be a middle-school guidance counselor's trifecta: divorce, mental illness, and addiction. In the mid-fifties, things were much simpler. Daddy drank a little, mom was feeling blue, divorce wasn't discussed. Instead of being scheduled for extensive therapy, I was deemed fit to be in charge of my six-year-old brother, Bobby, on our first unsupervised visit to see our father in Fort Myers, Florida.

The premise was that he'd gotten it together after years of attempting sobriety. He had a good job as a supervisor building water storage towers. He had a safe, clean place for us to stay only a block from the beach. Most important, he'd stopped drinking. He'd even stopped smoking and this was years before quitting was fashionable. Drunk or sober, my dad was a charmer, but I don't really think it took much charm to convince my mother that a summer free from two squabbling kids was a great idea. As far as I was concerned, anything was better than babysitting my brother while Mom worked double shifts as a nurse. Plus, I loved the beach. It was decided that the two of us would spend June and July with Dad. My Uncle Sonny was commissioned to drive us both ways. And so the adventure began.

Uncle Sonny was the only one of my father's eight siblings that my mother could tolerate. Raised in poverty in the Tennessee mountains, Sonny had developed into something of a Renaissance man. He dabbled in antiques, briefly owning his own store. He starred in several stellar productions at the Chattanooga Little Theater. He bred Chihuahuas. Hard times in the arts and the dog industry had forced him to turn to manual labor and work with my father's crew building an enormous tank just outside Fort Myers.

Uncle Sonny picked us up early one June morning and we were on our way. The first two hours of the trip, Sonny was the perfect escort. He loved to sing, especially show tunes. His favorites were from the Little Theater's long-running hit musical *Little Mary Sunshine.* Sonny had played one of the Canadian Mounties and had even received favorable notice in the *Chattanooga News Free Press*. We'd memorized all the words to the closing number before we hit Calhoun, Georgia.

After we'd worn ourselves out vocally, Sonny began chatting on his CB radio. We learned that we needed to preface any response to nearby truckers with a cheery "Kick it on" and that we were from "Choo Choo town" getting ready to pass through "Watermelon 500" (Atlanta). But the most important thing we learned was that Uncle Sonny needed constant stimulation to keep from falling asleep at the wheel. Years later I learned that Sonny suffered from narcolepsy. At the time all I knew was that my brother and I had been ripped from the safety of our home and catapulted into mortal danger on the rolling roads of Georgia.

During a quick gas station bathroom stop, Bobby and I decided that one of us would have to remain alert at all times. We would take turns every two hours, making sure that our driver didn't doze off and careen into a power-line pole. This was, however, going to be a serious problem. Neither of us was a veteran traveler and the rhythm of the road combined with no air conditioning was coma inducing. Still, terror is an excellent motivator and after stocking up on bottles of Coca Cola for the road, we agreed I'd take the first shift.

Since Lady Bird Johnson's beautification program

didn't begin until the mid-sixties, the highways in 1963 were still graced with billboards of varying sizes and shapes. As a beginning reader, I'd driven my mother crazy reading each and every giant advertisement I saw. On this fateful trip, I reverted to my childhood habit as a survival tactic.

"Look, Uncle Sonny. 'The Reptile House: Marvel at the two-headed snake. Yes, he's alive and twice as deadly.' I've never seen a two-headed snake, have you? Do you think both heads actually work? I mean do you think two-headed means two-brained?" I had to poke Sonny to get an answer; not good.

"'Kentucky Fried Chicken: It's finger lickin' good. Take home a ten-piece bucket today.' Ten pieces sounds like a lot, but I guess most families could eat that much. I can eat at least two and Bobby can eat three if two of them are drumsticks. Do you think the Colonel is a real colonel? I read somewhere it's an honorary title. Seems strange to me that you'd be honored for making chicken. It is good chicken, though. Don't you think it's good chicken, Uncle Sonny?" He turned toward me with glazed eyes and nodded.

"Hey, let's stop at Stuckey's! 'Every trip's a pleasure when you stop at Stuckey's.' There's one only 12 miles away. I could sure go for a delicious pecan log. Wouldn't you like a pecan log, Bobby? Hey, Bobby, I said a pecan log." Bobby was allergic to nuts, but he groaned gamely in agreement from the back seat.

We stopped at Stuckey's for pecan logs. We stopped for another three bathroom breaks. We stopped for Bobby to throw up pecan log. We stopped to let an armadillo amble across the road. We even stopped at the Stephen Foster House, now known as the Stephen Foster Culture Center State Park. We ate a fancy lunch there and Uncle Sonny browsed for antiques while Bobby and I sat under the shade of a huge old oak tree trying to plan our next move.

We had at least five more hours to go. There wasn't much hope my brother would make it farther without passing out, and I wasn't doing a whole lot better myself. I was almost desperate enough to call Mother to ask for advice, but I knew that would result in the cancellation of the entire trip. Stumped for a solution, we leaned back against the tree staring up at low hanging branches covered with Spanish moss, and we both fell into a sound sleep. Several hours later the buzzing of a bumble bee woke me. I shook Bobby into consciousness and together we set off looking for Uncle Sonny.

We found him sleeping peacefully with his head on his arms at a nearby picnic table. Just after we reached him, he came to and we resumed our journey. I rode shotgun with Bobby pulling my ponytail periodically to make sure I was alert. Sonny kept the CB radio blaring static and we reached our destination about 2:00 a.m.

Fort Myers was the perfect beach. We spent long, lazy days alternating between swimming in the ocean and fighting over TV shows in our motel room. We soon discovered that our father's definition of abstinence didn't completely jibe with ours. He didn't smoke anymore – cigarettes, that is. Cigars didn't count. He'd quit drinking the hard stuff, but wine wasn't even alcohol, not really. Every night he finished almost a gallon jug, passed out, and snored loudly while we stayed up as late as we wanted. Cigar smoke and Zinfandel fumes were small prices to pay for the independence and freedom of life almost on our own. We kept our secrets when we gave our weekly phone reports to Mom.

The only dark spot on our horizon was the specter of our return trip. A disagreement between my father and uncle over the latter's work ethic most likely saved our lives. Uncle Sonny went home three weeks early in a huff, leaving us without a driver.

Our parents decided we could handle an overnight bus trip, so at the end of July we boarded a Chattanooga-bound Greyhound. Dad must have slipped the driver a little something extra because he smiled at us reassuringly and guided us to seats right behind him.

"I bet this is your first big trip all by yourselves. No need to be scared. I haven't lost anybody yet?" He chuckled at his own joke, but seemed surprised at our enthusiastic reaction. We started giggling and couldn't stop until the bus had left the station. Then we curled up together and, for the next six hundred or so miles, slept.

-Kathy Nichols

Cold Comfort

I miss you so much…
I wish things were different
That we both felt the same
That you had answered my letter
Said you loved me too
I would be there right now, with you -
Helping you
Loving you
But you didn't…
I am here, you are there
Alone, struggling, unsure
All I can do is offer you words of
Encouragement
From a distance
Loving you is too painful
Wanting you too frustrating
Needing you futile – pointless
Some things just aren't meant to be
But in the wee hours of the night
And early in the morn
It is me you call for comfort
Cold comfort
Across telephone lines for tacit touch
Distant reassurances and infusions of hope
All of the trappings of love without love itself
How did it ever come to this?
How did I come to this place…
Where this shell, this farce, plays a poor imposter to love?
What I would not give to have the love
The life I have so long desired…
Why would God plant this hunger in my soul, and leave me
empty?
I have no answers only loneliness and longing, hunger and

unrequited passion.
I cannot go on like this much longer...
Every part of me is becoming brittle
Soon there will be nothing but the faint memory of desire
And that too will fade
Leaving a zaftig husk that will gratefully crumble
Returning to the dust
Free at last from the unrelenting, ravenous craving
For what has always... always eluded me.

Manna

Silvery pearls,
Delicate as dew,
Coated the tents and tough desert grasses.
With hands browned and weathered,
From Egypt's cruel yoke,
We gathered the gift –
This bread from heaven,
To feed the hunger that lingered
Unslaked
By liberation.
Though we feasted on honeyed cakes and quail,
Nothing satisfied.
The savory leeks of home
Were succulent in remembrance.
The taste lingered on our tongues,
Wiping away the bitter bite of the whip.
In the shadow of the Land of Promise
We recalled the cool Nile breezes
Cursed the desert heat
And longed for the familiar
Sting of subjugation.
Blind to miracle and wonder

We wandered
Impervious to the presence of the Almighty
Hovering cloudlike in our midst -
More real, more powerful
Than the parting Red Sea waters.
Manna
Pure and fine,
Was cast like pearls to swine.
Though many consumed,
Only the faithful few
Hungered
For the land of milk and honey.

-Lisa Stafford

F
A
L
L
Comes and leaves its mark.
Days are shorter, sooner dark.

Festivals create their fun:
Face-paint drying in the sun.

Cake Walks,
Pumpkins,
Pony rides:

A fleeting time to be
Outside.

-Lynda Holmes

HULA HOOPING

Arms,
Neck,
Legs,
Waist:
The hula hoop will find its place.

Move,
Sway,
Try to
Turn:
Work into the calorie burn.

One hoop,
Two,
Three, or
Four:
You may wish to add some more!

Round and
Round,
Count the
Spins:
Twenty, thirty, forty and ten.

-Lynda Holmes

In My Dreams

In my dreams I am small and cute like a pixie. I don't really know what a pixie is, but I've heard ladies talk about cute little girls, and they say they look like pixies. So in my dreams I look like one. I don't have bangs from when Mama cut my hair with dull doctor's scissors, putting masking tape across my forehead but getting them crooked anyway. Instead I have long straight brown hair like Laurie Partridge's, and I can braid it or wear it in a ponytail.

In my dreams I don't have anemia—that's what Mama calls it. Instead, I have plenty of red blood cells (or is it white blood cells? I don't remember). My nose doesn't bleed, and I don't get tired. The doctor doesn't suck my blood into a little tube. I'm not tall and skinny and weak, but strong and fast, but also small so that when I sit in my school desk my toes just touch the linoleum (I learned that word yesterday. I like to say it. Linoleum).

In my dreams I have a modern 1970's name, like Susan or Connie. And when I get off the school bus, the kids all run to meet me and ask me what's up. Everything I say is funny (or witty—that's what Mama says) and Kevin Moore wants to go with me because he's the cutest boy in the class, so it's only natural that he should go with a cute pixie girl like me. I know all the answers to the teacher's questions, so she asks me to entertain the class with a song on my electric keyboard like Laurie Partridge's.

I have my best dreams when I'm awake. My dreams help me go to sleep.

Today when I get off the school bus, I bring my new pencils that Uncle Stewart gave me. They are different colors and have my name written on them in gold: Emily Wells. They are so neat, even though I wish they said Susan Wells or Connie Wells. I'm going to give one to

Mandy Singletary. Then maybe she'll want to be best friends.

Mandy not only has a modern 1970's name, but she's cute like a pixie. Her long, light brown hair hangs behind her shoulders, and when she sits at her desk, her feet don't reach all the way to the floor. Mandy always wears pants to school (or shorts when it's hot). Her mother doesn't make her wear dresses on picture day. Her two older brothers teach her how to run and fight and throw rocks, so the boys at school like her. If Mandy would be my best friend, then Kevin Moore would want to go with me.

Mandy thinks the pencil is really neat.

At recess, Mandy says we're going to play *Kung Fu*. She always gets to be Grasshopper. I always have to be the bad guy. I thought since I gave her the pencil, we could change places, but Mandy says no because I can't do kung fu kicks. Sonya and Kim get to be Grasshopper's helpers and hold the bad guy so Grasshopper can kick him. I tighten my stomach muscles, but it still hurts. I don't like playing *Kung Fu*. I'm glad when the bell rings and we have to go back to class.

At home after school Mama hands me a dark green pill. She says it's a vitamin to make me less tired and make my nose stop bleeding. I don't know how to swallow a pill. When I chew it up, it's nasty.

Tonight before I go to sleep I dream I'm Grasshopper's helper and Grasshopper has been ambushed by bad guys. I step in and do my kung fu kicks on all the bad guys. Grasshopper thinks I'm such a kung fu expert that he asks me to be his partner, but I can't because I have to practice my music because I'm also a backup singer for the Partridge Family.

At school Mandy makes me mad. She asks me which boy I like, but I'm embarrassed to tell. She promises she won't tell anybody, so I say I like Kevin Moore. She goes right to Greg Floyd and tells him, and Greg tells Kevin. All through recess, Mandy and Greg sing, "Emily and Kevin sitting in a tree, K-I-S-S-I-N-G." Kevin tells them to shut up, but they don't, so then Kevin pushes Greg and says no amount of money is enough to pay him to kiss an ugly toad like me. My face gets hot. I try not to cry, but my throat tightens up. I wonder if Mandy will ever want to be my friend.

At lunch I sit with Julie Singletary and Linda Bennett. Julie wonders why I want to be friends with someone who lies to me and makes fun of me at recess. She says if she was me, she'd show Mandy Singletary the door. Show her the door. I think that's right witty.

At home while I'm eating my Oreos, my nose starts to bleed. Before I can get to the bathroom, blood's dripped on my favorite blouse with the squirrels and pine cones on it. I roll up a square of Charmin, wet it in the sink, and stick it under my upper lip to stop the bleeding. I soak my shirt in cold water. Then I lie down on the bed and turn on the radio. Tony Orlando is tying a yellow ribbon around an oak tree. I sleep through dinner.

At breakfast I dream Johnny Gage is rushing me to Rampart Hospital after discovering I've been bitten by a Rocky Mountain Spotted Fever tick. He blares the siren as he calls the hospital: "Rampart 51! Rampart 51!" But Mama tells me to eat my frosted flakes before I miss the bus. I chew up my green pill and go to school.

At recess Mandy, Kim and Sonya want to play *Kung Fu* and say I have to be the bad guy. But I tell Mandy I want to be Grasshopper for once. She says no, she's always Grasshopper, and Kim and Sonya are her helpers. I'm tired of Mandy Singletary. No matter what I do, she's mean to me. I tell her I'm tired of doing everything she says, and I'm tired of her kicking me, and I won't play *Kung Fu*, so she'll have to find another bad guy, so there.

133

Then Mandy kicks me in the stomach. I'm not ready for it, so I can't tighten my stomach muscles. Thank goodness I wasn't close to her, so she doesn't get me that hard, but still I double over. And that's when I see the little red spot on my new Converse All-Stars orange sneaker. I touch my nose and find blood on my fingers, and I think of Marsha Brady and the episode when Greg, Peter, and Bobby accidentally hit her face with the football. I yell, "Oh, my nose!" in perfect Marsha fashion as I cover my face with my hands. It's too bad my hair's so short because if it were long like Marsha's, I could give the injury more drama. Bent over with my hands cupped around my nose, I collect the blood and walk toward the teachers' tree. Mandy follows me, asking me to please not tell, she's so sorry, she didn't mean to, and I can be Grasshopper for the rest of recess if I want. But I know she meant to, and I don't care about being Grasshopper anymore.

At the teachers' tree, I have a nice cupful of blood in my palms. I find Mrs. Anderson's sandals and drop the blood to the sand, reddish brown splattering in front of her pink toenails. Blood's all over my face too. I must look like Johnny Gage's worst patient. I look at the teachers and say, "Mandy kicked me." I don't mention where.

Mrs. Anderson puts her handkerchief on my nose and walks me to the office. She tells Mandy to come too because she has some explaining to do. Mrs. Brown gets the rest of the kids inside. I moan a couple more "oh my noses," but I really don't need to because Mandy is so scared, she can't stop whining she didn't mean to and she's sorry.

I've heard there's a paddling machine in the principal's office.

In the office the secretary wraps a little piece of ice from the teachers' lounge in some tissue and puts it under my lip. Meanwhile, Mrs. Anderson tells the secretary what happened, and Mandy says it was an accident. It was not.

The secretary asks if I'd like a Coca Cola, and I say, "Yes, ma'am, I would like that very much, thank you." She smiles. I know she's thinking my Mama raised me right. She wipes my face with a wet paper towel before she lets me drink it. Then she tells Mrs. Anderson to take Mandy in to see the principal, so I get up and show Mandy the door.

When Mama comes, she whispers with the secretary and then with the principal and Mrs. Anderson. She tells them I'll be fine and thank you for calling. Mrs. Anderson leads Mandy up to me and nudges her. Mandy mumbles she's sorry. I tell her that's okay, even though it's really not. I try to give the bloody handkerchief back to Mrs. Anderson, but she says no, I can keep that.

In the car with Mama, I sit in the front seat with the window rolled down. I'm still sipping my Coca Cola. I ask Mama if Julie Singletary can come over to play after school one day. Mama says of course.

At bedtime I go right to sleep.

-Nancy Lawson Remler

Incognito

"Eat your raisin bran," Mama tells me as she shoves an apple and a banana in her purse. "You won't get anything else before lunch. Do you want a granola bar?"

"The banana's better."

She keeps the granola bar and hands me the banana. I hold it as I slurp on cereal from a Styrofoam bowl and white plastic spoon. Al Roker delivers the forecast via the television mounted to the wall as a father and two kids help themselves to the bagels and cream cheese.

"Hurry," Mama says, shifting her eyes toward the blue-smocked woman refilling the Cheerios dispenser. Then she catches herself in her nervousness and says, "You don't want to be late."

I shovel the rest of the raisin bran in my mouth. As we depart, the clerk behind the counter calls, "Thank you for staying with Hampton Inn."

My pleasure.

Mama drops me off at a school bus stop up the street, waving as she pulls the car away. I don't know the other students there, but several parents drop kids off on their way to work. I blend right in. I sit next to a girl with dark brown skin, her wooly hair pulled into a stiff ponytail. She smells like lotion and bacon.

To avoid the afternoon heat, the cross country team practices before school in the springtime, taking a two-mile run around campus and through the adjacent neighborhood—Westwood Heights. I work up a drenching sweat as I run past mothers jogging in their Nike sports bras and New Balance shoes. The automatic sprinkler systems make puddles in the street, which I run around so water won't seep through the holes of my Pay-Less sneakers. I pick up my pace so I'll have time for a shower before class.

"Hey, can I borrow your shampoo? I forgot mine."

I pop open the tiny bottle I swiped from the hotel maid's cart and pour a dab into Claire's palm. I'm running low. Maybe I can get more tomorrow or the next day.

The bell rings for first period. I shove the last of my banana in my mouth before putting my shoes back on.

"I thought you wore those jeans yesterday," says Claire.

"No, I wore my other pair," I lie.

English, then biology, then music, then history. The cafeteria serves soggy fish filet sandwiches with slaw and limp French fries. I hate frozen processed seafood. I eat every bite.

"Eww, how can you stand that stuff?" Claire asks, picking at her food.

"It's not so bad."

Algebra, then health, then drama club after school.

"Have you sold all your candy bars for the fund raiser?" asks Mr. Caldwell.

"Almost." I'm not really lying. Mama and I ate three of them, but I did sell the rest. Then we used the money to buy gas.

"Want to come to my house to work on our biology project?" Claire asks.

"I don't know. . ."

Tough decisions. Claire's family has a beautiful three bedroom with beige carpet. Her mom always serves snacks, and we can have the TV on while we study. But how will I get all the way back to meet Mama?

"If your mom's working, mine can take you home," Claire says.

"Well, okay."

I offer to write the paper if Claire will make the poster for the presentation. She jumps at that deal, since writing the paper is harder. Now I don't have to buy art

137

supplies.

"Looks like your mom's not home yet," Claire's mom says from behind the steering wheel. "Should we wait?"

"No need. I have a key to the back door." I hold up the brass keychain I've carried with me for the past six months.

"Thanks for the brownies and the ride."

I wave to them as I walk around the house, where I stay until the minivan pulls out of the driveway. Before leaving I peek in the windows, through the thin pink and white gingham curtains still hanging in my now empty bedroom. I turn the key—now useless—over in my fingers. I want to break in, just to sit on the floor for a while. But I'm afraid. No telling when an agent my appear to show the house.

I put my arms through the straps of my back pack and walk up the street toward DeRenne Avenue, where I'll meet Mama at the corner convenience store. At 6:30, the sun shines on my back. Sweat beads at my hair line, on my top lip, and under my arms. Mama's parked out front with the windows down. I sit in the passenger seat and discover she's spreading peanut butter on bread with a plastic knife.

"I bought this stuff inside. Do you want to use the restroom?"

I shake my head. I went at Claire's.

"Find anything today?"

Mama frowns and shakes her head.

"I applied at the paper mill—along with a hundred other people."

Then her face brightens.

"But I did find a nice hotel for us tonight."

Thank goodness for small blessings. We eat our sandwiches in the park and sit at the picnic table until after sunset, mosquitoes pricking at our arms and whining in our ears. By the time we get to the Best Western Southside, the moon's out. Mama pulls into a parking space in the back. "See this?" She's proud of her find. "The parking lot's a good distance from the main office, so no one will see us." She points out the window. "And the shade of this tree will block the morning sun."

Mama reclines the driver's seat, then reaches in the back for a pillow. She punches it before settling in and closes her eyes. I rest my head on the back of my seat and read the scrolling hotel marquis through the rear view mirror: "Free Continental Breakfast. . .HBO."

-Nancy Lawson Remler

The Other Half

I found the partner of that sock you lost
so long ago. Do you recall the pair?
The argyle set you purchased from Lacoste,
with a little green gator in a square?

I found it in a box that's filled with your
old things, mementos from a time when two
were still one and everything felt so pure.
I'm coming apart at the seams, it's true,

because I know you're never coming home.
Where do the socks go when they disappear
from the wash? Are they better off alone
or do they miss their other half? It's clear

this old sock and I share some common traits –
both so lonely, we're longing for our mates

-Jason Wright

The Harvest

A huge rock endures wind—cold—heat
   Until it finally breaks.
A seed finds its way into a crevice,
   Germinates, grows and breaks the rock again.
This is repeated many times.
The rock is gone, but life-giving soil remains.

A grain of corn is placed into the soil,
   Two leaves appear—then the stalk—and the ear
From this one kernel, one plant—two, three, maybe four
ears.
   Hundreds of kernels of corn. Food.

A tiny egg hatches,
   A worm crawls forth in search of food.
In time the worm builds itself a snug cocoon
   The cocoon bursts—releasing a beautiful butterfly.

Did the huge rock die—
   Or the grain of corn or the egg?
Each changed forms and for these we rejoice:
   The enriched soil.
      The bountiful food.
         The beauty of nature.

A child is born, he, too, withstands
   The winds of adversity,
      The coolness of a so-called friend,
         The heat of another's scorn.
Bearing adversity makes him stronger, truer, and more
courageous.
   Bearing his friend's coolness teaches him patience,
tolerance, truth.

Bearing another's scorn builds within—compassion,
kindness, forgiveness.

As was the rock, he may be broken many times;
    As does the seed, he produces food—fruits of the spirit.
        As does the worm, he has his struggle with life.
Yet, as the butterfly left its cocoon to soar to freedom,
    Man, too, leaves this useless shell behind and soars to
even greater freedom.

If you must grieve for me, grieve now, for
While I may waiver before the trials,
    While I may be humiliated by a so-called friend,
    While I may ache from unjust criticism,
When the battle is over and my body lies in repose:

REJOICE! For I, having left the useless cocoon to
deteriorate into dust,
    Will be in a much more beautiful state than any butterfly.
For having died many deaths, I will then be truly alive.

                                        -Nell McWilliams

Dinner Date

He's bragging again,
as if you were his mirror
for preening and posturing.

Just as you are about to speak,
he hushes you to hear
James Taylor on the radio.

Now, he says your kid
– the gifted one – reminds
him of himself at that age.

He extends his card
with a smile to the waitress
under the guise of business.

When he turns to maligning
his ex-wife as a castrating bitch,
you raise your glass in silent salute.

Zookeeper's Pantoum

as she paces before the bars
he keeps feeding her meaty tidbits
she looks for the way out
he wants to be close if only for a while

he keeps feeding her meaty tidbits
so she settles, accepting his offerings,
he wants to be close if only for a while
and she hungers for more

so she settles, accepting his offerings,
as she looks more closely at the cage
she hungers for more
he built these walls to keep just out of reach as she looks
more
closely at the cage
she realizes
he built these walls to keep just out of reach
she's free to walk away

she realizes
as she paces before the bars
she's free to walk away
she looks for the way out

-Phyllis McCoy Lightle

Ridge Road

Big Mama and Daddy Walt lived ten miles out,
out of Opelika, out of Pepperell Village, out on Ridge Road
where they bought twenty acres with what they earned
sweating out the '40s and '50s in the cotton mill
where their white frame house sat just off the blacktop
where mimosa trees welcomed with pink puffs extended
like gifts in the upturned hands of dancers
where my daddy came of age and struck out on his own
after giving the mill six months
of his last indoor labor
where he returned with my brother and me every Sunday he
could
where we played with cousins while grownups visited
inside
where we climbed trees barefoot

143

where we ducked under the plum tree's deeply-bowed
branches
in search of edible offerings
where we entertained ourselves around back at the catalpa
tree,
plucking fuzzy green and black worms,
a grandfather's fish bait but our delight
as they tickled backs of hands and arms
where we checked on the laying hens in their coop
where we steered clear of the pump house on the side
where the old well remained covered but still served up
stories
of rattlesnakes and curious missing dogs
where we finished our circuit around the yard
flopping on the front porch swing
where we waited for the call to wash for dinner
                                        -Phyllis McCoy
                                        Lightle

Old Teacher Man

As the cloud hugs the mountain
And the tea played in the paper cup
One cough inspired another
            in the Old Teacher Man.
The bell down the hall loves to ring
Air writes its own music as the
            nurse played with her toys.
The bed tested the man and his time
Trees talk to the wall while
            Old Teacher Man recites words of long ago.

                                        -Mary Reid

Arkansas Pine

I am from the towering pines sheltering me from the land
I was born of the tracks of trains, the rickety racket of the
engine
Of sunset - From out of Mrs. Ross' house - The house I see
across the street
From fox holes in the dark - The sound of the alarm coming
from the paper mill
Signaling fire - Where Daddy works the graveyard
Shift
From the smell of sulphur burning an etch in my DNA
As I lay
Scattered among books scattered about the floor - words I
cannot read
I am from those words and from the excitement of their
unknown stories
From Della the half-blind babysitter that tells me to shut the
doe
And so I do - I am from her and her doe.
From trailers and tornadoes, dip and spit, the chew that wastes
away in the nasty mouths of men – I am from their 18
wheelers and Cadillacs with Grand Ole' Opry vomit in back
From Faulkner and Williams, big hair and big mouths
I am of a dusty old Bible covered with beer cans and broken
doors
From the smell of the sun upon drunken skin – from ugly
floors and footstools
And the humidity of suppression repressing the beauty of an
internal poem left
Untouched in my mind – I am from a language of a people I
could never understand
Who speak out of the smoke and ash – a staleness that leaves
my breath behind
uncomfortable with a comfort nestled in a pine
- touching a cloud with its needle.

-Renee Basinger

Fly Me to the Moon

Jules Verne took the boy
on his first journey
from the Earth to the moon
in a Classics Illustrated comic book
bought for twenty-five cents
off the rack at the back
of Foster's Drug Store,
Main Street, Podunk, U.S.A.,
about as far as you could get
from the moon in those days
and still be on the planet Earth.

Back then all the boy knew
about the moon
was that it was a boon
to budding poets
because it rhymed with spoon and June
and had something to do with love
and silver light from up above.

He knew less about love
than he did about the moon,
and there was no book
on the rack for that,
no Jules Verne to tell the story,
show the way,
illustrate in pulp fiction
comic book color,
how to love,
how to allow himself to be loved,
how to fly to the moon
and, like Neal Armstrong,
come home again.

He had to learn
that lesson for himself,
like we all do,
or maybe like some of us
don't.

Poem Read Aloud

I am a figment
of your imagination,
exist only in the mind
and in precise
well-chosen words
that fashion
from airy nothingness
something you can see,
something you can hear,
smell, taste, almost feel,
like the bones
beneath the flesh
in the back of your hand
or the petals of a rose;
shadow, image,
lightning flash,
thought bubble cumulus cloud
drifting overhead
once the lamp is rubbed,
once the wick is set ablaze
and words summon
from airy nothingness
something.

                                        -Ron Self

Crossing the Fall Line

I distrust this hill country, where I can see
my destination up among trees
high and dense like nodules of moss,
straight ahead as the eagle flies,
if only I could.

Between there and here
four lanes of blacktop diverge
then disappear.

The seven hills of this Rome trap the uninitiated,
hemming us in at the foot of Appalachia
so we drive in circles,
homesick,
unable to solve the labyrinth.

If I can escape this knotted land and head south—
just find the through-line out—
hills will calm like ocean after a storm.

Mid-state the land falls away level,
pressed flat by the weight of an ancient sea.
I've crossed the fall line before.

Brain and lungs resolve in sudden space.
Walls recede. Views lengthen like afternoon shadows.
I can point myself toward any destination I see,
or the horizon itself,
and just go.

-Sandra Giles

First Memory

A brief image, striped
through white crib bars,
dim light from down the hall
and the shadow of someone
walking away.

The child who sleeps risks forgetting.
But to stay awake,
contemplating shadows through bars,
courts a deeper cost.

Still, it is not fear or loss
I'm trying to tell you,
but mystery, the comfort
of solitude,
a chiaroscuro of leaving.

At the Aquarium

As the seahorse drapes his tail around a sturdy stalk
to prevent drifting aimlessly through the element of water,
to anchor himself so he may stay with us,
touching what is rooted in earth,
so I cling to you,
that I might be staid, present
amidst the whirlpool of language,
the whirlwind of intellect,
which tempt me from the passion of simple things:
a smile, a touch,
your arm as you offer it.

-Sandra Giles

Just Past the Yellow Sign

I remember my immortal father: the man who was taller and stronger than anyone else's father; the one who could lift my three-year-old frame over his head; the one who yelled at me with the fire of an angry Zeus for playing with fire. I remember thinking of him as invincible. I never saw him sick or hurt, and every morning he woke up earlier than my young brain could imagine just to go to work so I could continue singing into toy microphones on the hearth—a habit that would culminate in hours of drunken karaoke as I got older.

When I was a kid, my parents bought me a Big Wheels Monster Truck, and they would only let me drive it on the road when my dad walked with me. He had to be there to protect me, or my overprotective mother would lose her shit. There was this yellow sign that he would never let me drive past. "Let's turn around, Tadpole," he would call out as I reached the yellow diamond that marked the end of the track. And I would turn as fast as my plastic wheels and four small batteries would let me, hearing the slow rev of the little motor, and we would be on our way back home.

I remember the first time I hurt him. I was a fan of professional wrestling when I was young, and my father and I would wrestle in the living room floor. He was always on his knees to alleviate the unfair advantage that his size gave him. One afternoon as he was lying on the couch, I decided I would unleash a ferocious surprise attack and drop an elbow on him. That elbow came down in his eye, blackening it like a battle wound from a war he didn't even know he was fighting. He jumped from the couch yelling things that I can't remember probably because I had never heard the words before. And I was upset because I had hurt the unhurtable. God was becoming more human.

I awoke late one night when I was in middle school. I could hear gasping from the next room—the sound of a closed throat struggling to find air. My room was across the hall from my parents', and I watched my mother try to calm him down so he could breathe again. There were doctor appointments and medicines, and I'm not sure what eventually stopped those horrific gasps, I just remember watching as the invincible became more vulnerable.

Then, in graduate school, my always-supportive parents drove to visit me in the classroom left in my hands as a teaching assistant. After a quarter-mile walk from the parking lot and fifteen stairs, my father sat down, hand-on-knee, to rest—breathing deeply. Gods don't have to rest. Gods ascend stairs with ease. A few moments later, he stood and climbed the rest of the way.

Two weeks later, my mother and I stand on either side of a hospital bed in the recovery unit of a cardiovascular center. The beeping was so loud. I couldn't stand the way it sounded. And there was a similar beeping coming from every single room around the perimeter of the floor. And even though I knew that constant beeping was better than one long beep, it was impossible to find comfort in the beep's persistence.

I studied the numbers on the monitor: heart rate, blood-oxygen level, temperature. What did they all mean? It all seems so arbitrary—a meaningless measuring system used to confuse those of us who were liberal arts majors in college. Maybe it's the med student's revenge for all of the plays we got to perform, music we got to hear, and poetry we got to read while they were learning symptoms and treatments. Maybe.

He awoke briefly, and I could tell he didn't recognize me. He just wanted the tube out of his throat. He was groggy and didn't have the strength to retrieve it as he had hoped he would, but he tried. And I wished more than

151

anything that I could have made him relax so they could take it out, but he couldn't hear me. I looked at my father, struggling to retrieve the breathing tube, and as he slowed his flailing, and his eyes came to rest on mine, I saw a single tear fall from the corner of his left eye and slide slowly down his cheek, filling in the wrinkles like tributaries.

Only a few weeks after the five bypasses, I was walking with him in the old neighborhood where I grew up and he still lived with my mother, across the street from the creepy poodle lady who walks her dog at night as an excuse to peep in windows. He worked hard to get his walking speed and distance back up, but he never pushed himself too hard. "How far are we walking today?" I would ask. "Just past the yellow sign," was his response. I was happy to walk every step with him because he walked every step with me. And as we moved just a few feet past the yellow sign, I would call out, "Let's head back," and we would, knowing all the time that it was these walks that we shared that made us so close. And I walked alongside my father as he descended the gentle slope from the yellow sign to home, seeing him as a god descending Olympus to earth, to live out the rest of his life—finally human in my eyes. And I felt like he was worthy less of praise and worship, but more of love and compassion.

-Shane Wilson

Merry Christmas, Mr. Crowe

There was one Christmas card left in the box when Belle finished her Christmas card list. It seemed a shame not to send the last card. But who else did she know that she could send a card to? Taking the thin phone book, she began scanning the entries. Beginning at the A's, she glanced down through the list. She knew the Arnolds but so did everyone else. They would surely have many Christmas cards. The Abneys had moved to Richmond recently and Belle did not have their new address. The Beckleys were popular throughout the county; no doubt their mantle would be crowded with cards. The Calamis owned the grocery store; everyone would send them a card.

Her eyes fell on the name Ernest Crowe, Covey Road. Now there was a man who could stand some cheering up, she thought. Since his wife died, he was like a specter moving slowly around town, walking to the post office or the store. Muttering when a neighbor spoke to him, he never had a real conversation with anyone that she ever saw. Even at his church, she had heard he arrived late and moved out slowly and silently just before the last amen was said.

Belle pondered about how to sign the card finally deciding to simply write Merry Christmas, Belle Hubbard. She tucked the card into the envelope and licked it. Putting the stamps on all 25 cards made Belle smile with her accomplishment, it was only the day after Thanksgiving. Her heart felt less lonely now that she had shared some Christmas cheer with friends.

Several days later Tassie popped into Mr. Crowe's front door and shouted, "Papa, here's the mail. Mom says we can't stay today she has a PTA meeting tonight and we got to cook Daddy some supper before she goes. See ya tomorrow." The door slammed before the mail dropped on

153

the dining room table. Mr. Crowe slowly moved toward the table, tugged on the pull cord to turn on the single light bulb overhead and picked up the new pile of mail that joined yesterday's and the day before's. Holding it in one hand, he shuffled through the mail muttering to himself. A large crisp white envelope stood out from the other regular sized ones. "A Christmas card, I bet," he said.

Reaching into his overalls pocket for his knife, he slit the envelope open. He slowly pulled the card out. The crisp white card had a carriage house in a snow scene with a horse drawn buggy and a man and woman warmly dressed. "Merry Christmas to you and yours," Mr. Crowe mumbled under his breath. "I should just scratch through the *and yours* part. 'Cause there ain't no *and yours* here. " He stirred around on the dining room table long enough to find an ink pen and then marked through the words *and yours* on the card's front. Opening the card he read the message aloud, "May the joy of the season be with you through the New Year. Merry Christmas, Belle Hubbard. Hum." He threw the card on the table and walked into the kitchen to eat his supper – cold biscuits and Spam.

Slipping out of his overalls, he washed his face and hands in the wash basin and walked to the bedroom. The temperature seemed especially cold tonight, but he decided to get another quilt from the oaken wardrobe and not add any more coal to the fire. He laid the covers back and slid his thin, lanky body into the bed. After reading a chapter from the Book of Proverbs, he reached for his ledger and wrote:

High temperature 32 F./low temperature 22 F.

Found at Carhartt - two handfuls of brass buttons, 8 metal zippers, 12 cardboard spools

Folks seen while walking home – Butch Hardy, Preacher Arvin, Brother Deitch

News- McNamara warns Johnson that communists

154

are gaining strength in South Vietnam,
        Portions of New York State and other New England
states still have power failure
        Christmas card from Belle Hubbard

He closed his ledger. Pulling on the long string connected to the light pull which he had tied to the bedpost, he turned out the light and went to sleep.

Several days later Belle was listening to WIRV while she washed the dishes. "Welcome, you're on the Trading Post," Belle heard the radio announcer say. She listened every morning from 9 until 10 while folks traded, sold and gave away different items. It was silly but she enjoyed the company while she baked and cleaned in her bright white and blue kitchen. The oven's heat made the kitchen cozy so she decided to sit and have a second cup of coffee after she put the last layer of the Wash Day Cake into the oven. By the time she finished her coffee, the apples would be ready to be mashed and put on the cake. Then the load of whites would be ready to be wrung out and hung up. The ring of the phone startled Belle.

"Hello," she said.

There was a long silence. "Hello is anyone there?" she asked.

"Yes," a low man's voice replied. "I wanted to huh, I wanted to call and say thank you for the Christmas card. It was very," he phased, "it was very cheerful. I am glad you sent it to me." He fumbled with the card in his hand while he talked.

"You're most welcome, Mr. Crowe. I wanted to share some Christmas cheer. I haven't seen much of you lately. Are you fairing well?" she asked and then regretted it.

"I'm doing OK for an old man, I guess. I've been working on the wooden silverware trays I give all the

155

grandkids when they get married. It's too cold to work in my shop so I brought my tools into the living room and I'm been working on those in the morning before I go to Carhartts," he said.

"That's nice. I bet the grandkids enjoy them. How many married grandkids do you have? Albert and I were never blessed with grandchildren," she said.

"Let's see only Tim and Pat's got married so far but I s'pect that Tassie be married soon," he said.

"Mr. Crowe, why, Tassie can't be more than 8 years old. You know better," she giggled awhile before she could speak again. "I know she is good company to you."

"Belle, I'd like to have your company. Could you have supper with me on Friday?" he blurted it out.

"Why, Mr. Crowe, I would love to have supper with you on Friday."

"I'll come by 'bout 4:30 and we can walk to the Wigwag. Will that do you?"

"Yes, Mr. Crowe, that will do me nicely. See you then."

-Mary Reid

The First Time in Years

Sophie awoke and stared at her surroundings: a cardboard box for a room, a worn-out fleece jacket for a pillow, and a bath towel for a blanket. Well, today was the end of her adventure. She had five dollars left. Sue's baby needed formula and Carry's little boy had no shoes. The sound of sirens in the distance had no impact on Sophie. They were common in this part of town. She stood, stretched, yawned, and began to make her way through the rubble toward Sue and her baby girl. Sensing someone behind her she turned and looked into the face of a stern policeman.

"Are you Sophie Maddock?" he asked, glaring at her.

"Yes," she answered, looking down. She glanced around and saw Sue and Carry watching her with question marks in their eyes.

"Come with me," he said. Taking her by the arm, he led her back out of the narrow alley onto a street where men and women in business suits went about their daily business.

"Am I in trouble?"

"I don't know," answered the cop. "Your husband has reported you missing, and a lot of people have been looking for you. So far as I know, you haven't broken any laws, so you're not being arrested at this time."

"Good," said Sophie. "I didn't realize anyone was looking for me."

The officer looked startled. "If my wife had been gone two weeks, I'd certainly be out looking for her. You've got a lot of explaining to do, so you'd better come along with me to the station. Your husband is waiting there."

Sophie accompanied the officer back to his car. Two weeks? It couldn't have been that long. It seemed more like two days. But then, maybe it had. She looked closely at the calendar date on her watch: September 16.

The Sunday before Labor Day, the mall had a big sale. Since Charles was working and Sophie was lonely, she decided to go to the mall. In the parking lot, she found a brown envelope. She opened it and inside was a large amount of cash. After an unsuccessful attempt to find the owner, she finished shopping and left. Driving through downtown she saw many homeless, hungry people in the streets. Charles would not be home until late and would be up and at work again before she arose, even though it was a holiday. Charles was like that. He always had a goal, something he had to do. As she watched the street people, she remembered the money. Maybe she could help these people. The money was not really hers. She parked and went into a little sandwich shop and bought ten sandwiches. When she reached into the envelope for money, she realized there was much more than she'd originally thought. She walked down the street and approached some women standing on the steps of an old church building.

"Are any of you hungry?" she asked. "I have some sandwiches."

Before she could get the sandwiches out of the bag, their hands had grabbed them. Almost embarrassed for the women as they snatched at the food and gulped it down, she sat down on the steps with them and ate a sandwich herself. She wanted to be one of them.

"My name is Sophie," she said.

"Mine's Emily," said one girl. Emily had flaming red hair, and she introduced the others.

Gradually Sophie learned that some of them had a place to live, and others lived on the streets. Some had jobs, some part-time jobs, and some had no jobs at all. After they finished the sandwiches and disposed of the wrappers in a nearby trashcan, they began to walk down the street and Sophie walked with them. She was intrigued by their closeness and the way they supported one another. They walked down into a little alley that had several cardboard "shacks" set up to sleep in.

"Welcome to our condos," said Sue, a young woman with a three or four month-old baby girl on her hip. Sophie smiled and sat on an orange crate.

"What's your name?" said a little boy, approaching from behind Sophie. She had not noticed him before. She introduced herself and fell instantly in love with him. She learned that his mother was Carrie. He clung to one of the sandwiches his mother had saved for him.

She talked and talked to these young women, and before long it was night, and they asked her to stay, and she did. The next day, she used some more of her money to buy food, and to take one of the kids to the doctor. And the next day and the next, needs kept mounting and she found new people with new needs, and the day would end and she would be exhausted.

And finally here she was at the end of her money. And the needs were still there. And now the policeman had arrived to take her home. She was sad.

"May I speak with them for just a minute?" Sophie asked, indicating Carrie and Sue, who had come to the edge of the alley and were watching her as she talked to the policeman.

"Sure," he said. "As I said before, you're not under arrest, but I would like to take you back to the station to meet your husband."

"Are you in trouble with the law?" her friends asked as she approached.

"Not really, but I have to leave," she said. She smiled a bit shyly. "My husband is looking for me."

The two women looked at each other. Their eyes grew wide. "Will you come back?" they asked in unison.

"I hope so. I need your friendship," Sophie said quietly.

"You've given us so much the last few days," said Sue. "How can we repay you?"

"You don't need to repay me," said Sophie. "You've given me something, too. Your friendship, a sense of community, and a purpose. I need to repay you. I promise to do so soon."

As Sophie settled into the police car, she wondered how she would explain her experience to Charles. He would probably never understand. He might be angry at her. He might even laugh at her. She smiled. It didn't really matter. In the end he'd accept her for who she was. She felt a sense of purpose for the first time in many years.

-Merrill J. Davies

The Journey

Lewis had been given more kindness the past eighteen months than in all his sixteen years before coming to the youth detention center. The judge who sentenced him was a kind man. The counselor who ignored his belligerent behavior was a kind man.

Oh, there were a few foster parents he lived with over the eight years before coming to the center who tried to be kind to him. But he always ended back in the Children's Home when they, one by one, gave up trying to help him.

> "When he got up that morning, everything was different. He enjoyed the bright spring day. But he did not realize it exactly, he just enjoyed it."

Lewis wished his counselor, Jerry Black, was here this morning. He wanted to see him one more time before he took the train back to his home town. Jerry Black had said good- bye the evening before. As they shook hands Jerry clasped his shoulder, looked him in the eyes and said, "You can do it. Remember you have choices."

Over the past eighteen months Jerry Black had spent so much time with him, helping him to understand that he was not responsible for his parents' behaviors; that if he could let go of all the anger, guilt and frustration, there was hope for him. He did not have to grow into the angry, violent man his father had been, or the weak, cowering person his abused mother had become as she reminded him every day, "You are bad".

All the "badness" reared up on the day he lashed out at the boys teasing him in the high school gym. The destruction

161

he caused with one of the iron poles that held weight lifting disks was too awful to contemplate. He was lucky that no one was killed that day and that the two guys who ended up in the hospital survived. Sixteen years of rage is pretty powerful.

Lewis had a tightening in his chest as he picked up the small blue duffle bag. He was on his way to Mr. and Mrs. Earls' home. He would live in their home and work in Mr. Earls' shop. Jerry Black told him stories of other fellows who had benefited from the kindness of the Earls. The tightness in his chest grew stronger. He felt like crying. He had not cried since he was eight years old when his father burned his hand for crying and had screamed at him, "Men in this town don't cry".

In Jerry Black's counseling sessions Lewis had learned the other guys had grandfathers and fathers who were violent. As Mr. Black peeled away layer after layer of hurt and misplaced guilt, he told them it would take a life time; it was like pealing an onion, layer by layer until you get to the core. But it could be done. He helped them practice all sorts of techniques to focus the mind away from the past and down to the present moment. Jerry Black's favorite line as he closed each session was "'the past is gone; you don't know the future; you have only this moment. What will you do with this moment?"

Lewis waited for the train that would take him to his new life. He felt alone. What if Mr. or Mrs. Earls did not like him? What if he became so frustrated that his anger erupted again? Even though he had spent the past eighteen months learning to curb his anger he did not do it alone. His counselor was always there encouraging him and showing

162

him a range of choices. Most important, he helped Lewis understand the consequences of choices made in haste.

The train finally arrived at the station. Passengers boarded, found seats and settled in for the trip. Some opened books and started reading; others simply gazed out the window and watched the scenery as the train picked up speed and moved across country.

Lewis finally relaxed enough to remember Mr. Black had handed him a small book as he said goodbye. He had pushed it into the duffle bag without looking at it. Now, as he tried to hold back tears and concentrate on relaxing the tightness in his chest, he reached into the duffle bag and looked at the book, *Leaves of Grass* by Walt Whitman.

Lewis held the book in his hand and stared down at the cover. He had never owned a book. He would treasure this gift. A small square of blue paper was tucked inside the book and an arrow drawn on the paper pointed to a poem, "I sit and look out".

For a moment Lewis' mind went back to the last weeks at the center. Mr. Black had started reading short poems to the group. He had encouraged them to read poetry, and one evening, he had them writing a poem. There was much laughter at their feeble efforts.

Now, as he read a poet describing the sorrows of the world, Lewis started to cry. Embarrassed, he held the newspaper in front of his face until he could get control. The longer he read, the more relaxed he felt, and by the time he saw Mr. Earls at the train station, he had a smile on his face.

Years later, standing in front of a large audience, Lewis looked out into the face of his own son. When he had finished reading from his latest book of poetry, Lewis made his way through the crowd to his wife and son. Holding a well worn and a bit tattered book in his hand, he pulled his family into the circle of his arms and smiled as the sound of the applause echoed around them.

-Ellouise Connolly

White Lies, Like Snowflakes

"Are you okay?" he asks. "Honey, I'm fine,"
she says as salt water wells in her eyes.
Honey, I'm fine – it's just another lie
she tells him, a little white one this time.

"You aren't eating and haven't touched your wine."
"I'm tired that's all" is her only reply.
She picks at her food, trying not to cry
about the test with the bright blue plus sign.

"Don't worry about me. I'll be okay."
White lies dance, just like snowflakes in the air,
onto an avalanche of deceit. Snow
flurries swirl. They will bury her one day,

because the evidence of her affair
will show when her belly begins to grow.

-Jason Wright

Daddy

(Teacher model of an assignment to write a poem based on
"Papa Who Wakes up Tired in the Dark" from *The House
on Mango Stree*t by Sandra Cisneros)

How bravely you fought the enemy.
You, who had served in WWII in France
And admired Eisenhower.
You went to Korea in the '50's
To fight again.

Decades later, armed with a can of Lysol,
Your only weapon to fight the enemy—
The cancer attacking Mommy—
You met everyone at the door with your weapon
And sprayed them.

You tried to relieve the discomfort
Caused by the tumor in her abdomen—
Fleet will forever symbolize love to me—
But you lost your war, so you surrendered
And soon followed.

-Patsy Hamby

So Many Miracles

So many miracles, life does comprise,
As we would see, had we only the eyes;
So many miracles, with smiles or tears,
As we would hear, had we only the ears;
So many miracles, which truly are real,
As we would touch, had we only the feel;
So many miracles, with faith playing its part,
As we would know, had we only the heart.

                                        -Eugene F Elander

Art & Photo Gallery

Diane Osborne Yates Mill Pond

Alisha White Lizard on Bamboo

167

Peggy Albers The Guardian

Kristen Hansen Tintern

Kristen Hansen Thames Path

168

Kathleen McKenzie Western Jekyll Sunset

Alisha White Butterfly

Alisha White Lizard on Birdhouse

169

William South Contemplation

Barbara Lipe Eiffel Details

Kristen Hansen Bath

170

Patricia Gerard Savannah Statue

Betsy Hollis-Frey Artistic Dogwood

Brandi Mazesticeon-Hamson - Waterfall
Pine Mountain Trail, Pine Mountain, GA

Kathleen McKenzie New Day on Jekyll

Sidney Wilson The Old Church

172

Patricia Gerard Savannah Cemetery

Herb Cawthorne Azaleas

Geri M. Davis SWtheCloudCrowd

173

Kathleen McKenzie Jekyll Island Sunrise

Sidney Wilson Mountain Castle

Patricia Gerard Savannah Fountain

174

Geri M. Davis Only in Venice

Sidney Wilson Southern Winter

175

Roseanne Marie Peters Descanso Gardens

Teresa McCullohs Watermelon Delight

Geri M. Davis The Art Lesson

Diane Osborne For Cotton

Sidney Wilson Ice Queen's Cave

Herb Cawthorne Clematis

Roseanne Marie Peters Bill brought me roses

Diane Osborne Touching Trumpets

Diane Osborne Wash Day Break

Diane Osborne In Hog Heaven

Teresa McCullohs Let Sleeping Dogs Lie

Teresa McCullohs Roadside Graveyard

Diane Osborne West Georgia Sunset

Brandi Mazesticeon-Hamson Horseshoe Rock

Peggy Albers Amidst the Carrot Field

The Four Editors

Jean B. Copland teaches World Literature Online with ETROY, a Global University, Troy, Alabama. Published works include poetry, articles, and reviews in various publications: The *English Journal, Chattahoochee Review, Oconee Living,* and *Reach of Song* and a book, *Grandma's Legacy and Other Poems.* She has served as General Editor for *Shout Them from the Mountain Tops: Georgia Poems, 2003* and *Shout them from the Mountain Tops II: Georgia Poems and Stories with Art & Photos,* 2012, both sponsored by the Georgia Council of Teachers of English. She is presently working on a poetry collection with both original and previously published works.

Jean Copland

Hildegard Holmes

Hildegard K. Holmes has published several books of poetry and her autobiography, *We Made It Work.* Some of her poems have appeared in various publications, among them, *Shout Them from the Mountain Tops: Georgia Poems* and *Reach of Song.* Her latest collection of poetry, *Two Worlds, One Life,* tells the story of her life in Germany before and during World War, II and in the United States. She is a proud, active member of both the National League of American Pen Women and the Georgia Poetry Society. Most importantly, she is mother to three children and Oma to her five grandchildren.

Jane Dillard Knight, an ardent conservationist and an enthusiastic naturalist, has published a nature book, *Through My Watching Window: Wings and Other Nature Things.* She is an active member of the Columbus Audubon Society and Lynn Haven Wildlife Garden Club. She has published poetry *in Shout Them from the Mountain Tops: Georgia Poems*; also, in *Shout Them from the Mountain Tops: Georgia Poems and Stories with Art and Photos.* She has three children, eight grandchildren, and three great grandchildren.

Jane D. Knight

John S. Knight, Jr.

John S. Knight, Jr. is a native Georgian. He is an honors graduate of the Journalism School at the University of Georgia. He lives in Columbus with his beautiful and talented wife, Elizabeth. He is proud to be lifelong friends of fellow editor Dr. Jean B. Copland and her gifted son, Dr. John A. Copland, III. Having enjoyed writing and photography from an early age, John was delighted to be an editor for Shout I. He continues to use the skills he acquired from working in printing and publishing for over 25 years by being an editor of Shout II. His first novel is nearing completion and a book of poetry and photography is soon to follow.